Low
Cholesterol
C U I S I N E

Designer: Ivy Hansen

ACKNOWLEDGEMENTS
The publisher would like to thank the
following for loaning cutlery, glassware and
tableware for the photography of this book:

Dansab Pty Ltd for tableware (pages 18, 25,
38, 46, 61, 90)
Gero Pty Ltd for cutlery (pages 16, 46, 62)
Villeroy and Boch (Aust) Pty Ltd for tableware
(pages 62, 70, 85, 92)

Published by Bay Books
61–69 Anzac Parade
Kensington NSW 2033
National Library of Australia
Card number and ISBN 1 86256 296 2

BB88

Typeset by Savage Type Pty Ltd, Brisbane
Printed in Singapore by Toppan

Photography Per Ericson
Food styling Susan Whitter

MARGARET GEE'S *Low Cholesterol*
CUISINE

BAY BOOKS
Sydney & London

CONTENTS

A Taste of Japan: Sushi Rice • Cucumber Roll • Tuna Roll • Nigiri Sushi • Chicken and Vegetable Soup • Tofu and Noodle Soup • Miso Soup • Dashi Stock • Chicken Yakitori • Shabu Shabu • Chicken Tonkatsu • Cold Noodles with Nori • Spinach Salad • Seaweed Salad • Vegetarian Tempura • Grilled Garfish • Prawn Tempura • Beef Teriyaki • Chicken with Rice • Mushroom Salad •

Aromatic Dishes from India: Tandoori Chicken • Cauliflower with Yoghurt • Kitcheri • Pakoras • Beef Koftas • Dhal • Vegetable Samosas • Prawn Curry • Favourite Fish Curry • Taj Mahal Chicken • Punjab Potato Puree • Rajasthani Rice • Cardamom Fruit Salad • Raita • Bananas with Lemon • Hot Beef Vindaloo • Wholemeal Chapatis • Aviyal Mixed Vegetables • Peas and Beans in Spicy Tomato Sauce • Braised Cabbage with Cumin • Lassi • Chilli Chutney •

Pritikin-style Chinese Cuisine: Basic Chinese Chicken Stock • Mongolian Hot Pot • Chicken and Sweet Corn Soup • Beef in Black Bean Sauce • Hot and Sour Soup • Chicken and Mushroom Soup • Ginger Turnip Soup • Fish with Mangoes • Steamed Whole Szechuan Fish • Steamed Ginger Prawns • Stir-fried Squid with Broccoli • Steamed Whole Crab • Spring Rolls • Lemon Chicken • Lobster with Black Bean Sauce • Pineapple Chicken with Tangerine Peel • Red-cooked Chicken • Steamed Chicken and Broccoli • Chicken and Snow Peas • Chinese Chicken with Plum Sauce • Cucumber in Black Bean Sauce • Onion Egg Foo Yong • Buddhist Mushrooms • Szechuan Steamed Eggplant • Pritikin-style Chinese Dipping Sauces • Soy/ Ginger Dip • Soy/Mustard Dip • Soy/Chinese Wine or Dry Sherry Dip • Soy/ Sesame Dip • Soy/Lemon Dip • Soy/Pineapple Dip • Soy/Chilli Dip • Chinese Vegetable Crudites • Beijing Fruit Salad • Lemon and Orange Twists • Shallot Curls • Carrot Cutouts • Radish Roses • Fresh Flowers •

Distinctive Dishes from Vietnam: Prawn Soup with Rice Vermicelli • Beef with Bamboo Shoots • White-cooked Carrots with Sweet and Sour Sauce • Steamed Fish and Mushrooms • Chicken and Lemon Grass •

FAVOURITES FOR ALL OCCASIONS 76

Sensational Sandwiches: Gourmet Sandwich Combinations • Pineapple Ginger Spread • Salmon Spread • Zesty Cheese Spread • Great Grates •

The Great Outdoors: Honiara Marinated Fish • Delicious Jacket Potatoes • Marinated Mushrooms • Peppery Pumpkin Soup • Steamed Chicken and Tomatoes • Chicken and Apricot Stew • Rosemary Chicken Fillets • Chilli Prawns • Garlic Rolls • Wholemeal Chive Damper • Thai Chicken Fritters • Sizzling Beef with Barbecue Sauce • Crispy Calamari • Campfire Beans • Green Rice Salad • Brussels Sprouts Salad • Beetroot and Green Pea Salad • Potato, Celery and Radish Salad •

Christmas Cheer: Christmas Turkey • Sage and Raisin Stuffing • Herbed Roast Potatoes and Pumpkin • Prune and Onion Stuffing • Warm Christmas Rice • Broccoli with Cheese Sauce • Mexican Relish • Beans in Savoury Sauce • Steamed Christmas Pudding • Christmas Cake • Ricotta Whip •

Food for Children: Fruit Kebabs • Spicy Vegetable Kebabs • Banana Hot Dogs • Celery Sharks • Easy Vegetarian Pizza • Healthy Hamburgers • Real Potato Chips • Beef Kebabs in Black Bean Sauce • Vegetable Egg Scramble • Sandwich Meat Loaf • Paradise Dessert • Banana Raisin Milkshake • Strawberry Milkshake • Muesli Bars •

Treats: Special Banana Cake • Spicy Oat Loaf • Apricot Cake • Pineapple Cake •

ENJOY GOURMET FOOD PRITIKIN-STYLE

The Chinese have a proverb: food is the first happiness. How right they are. Gourmet food prepared the Pritikin way is a top taste cuisine that's naturally healthy and low in cholesterol.

For this book, I have adapted my favourite recipes from around the world to the lifesaving Pritikin-style cooking methods.

Enjoy pasta, spring rolls, moussaka, chicken cacciatore, French onion soup, Mongolian hot pot, prawn curry, falafel, delicious fruit crepes and other favourites from Europe and Asia, knowing that the recipes are based solely on those Pritikin principles of no added fat, oil, salt or sugar.

The essence of any cuisine lies in the herbs and spices of a particular part of the world, plus the freshest of ingredients. The secret of Pritikin preparation techniques is to stir-fry or saute in a little water or stock. Even those recipes traditionally fried will taste just as delicious — or even more so — oven baked or cooked in a non-stick pan.

The Pritikin program is not about denial. It is about enjoyment. Enjoying your food, your health and a wonderfully varied diet based on fresh fruit and vegetables, whole grains and small portions of protein foods.

I have been cooking Pritikin-style food for many years now, and I know how easy it is to enjoy the style of French cuisine, the charm of an Italian meal or the indulgence of a Chinese banquet — without harmful dietary effects.

Long may you enjoy your food and your health.

Margaret Gee.

PRITIKIN-STYLE PREPARATION HINTS

- ☐ When cooking poultry remove all skin and visible fat.
- ☐ For extra crisp roast vegetables, peel, slice, sprinkle with water and place in freezer for about 8 minutes. This helps potato and pumpkin in particular to brown and crisp to perfection.
- ☐ If a conventional recipe includes cream, low-fat yoghurt is a great substitute.
- ☐ Some non-stick cookware still occasionally causes 'sticking' problems, so line cake tins with foil before pouring in mixture.
- ☐ Some Pritikin-style cakes are slightly 'heavy' the day they are cooked. They taste better if refrigerated and eaten the next day.
- ☐ Two or three tomatoes whizzed up in the blender give an instant tomato puree.
- ☐ For barbecues, marinate overnight seafood, chicken or meat with salt-reduced soy sauce, dry red or white wine, fruit juice and herbs for extra flavour.
- ☐ Save water used to boil or steam vegetables for soups and sauces.
- ☐ Fresh lemon, orange or pineapple juice sprinkled will revitalise almost any Pritikin-style foods which seem too dry.
- ☐ Puree fresh fruit in blender for instant jam.
- ☐ Grated Geska (sapsago) cheese in small quantities will sharpen up any standard recipe which requires tasty cheese.
- ☐ Always preheat non-stick frypan before adding ingredients, especially for Asian dishes.
- ☐ My favourite fresh marmalade recipe is to blend together ½ lemon, 1 whole orange and 1 tablespoon of apple juice concentrate.
- ☐ Make breadcrumbs out of leftover Pritikin bread by blending for a few seconds. Pritikin bread and rolls are now available at many food stores and most supermarkets. The Pritikin cinnamon fruit bread is also delicious.
- ☐ A delicious flour can be made by blending raw oats until they become fine flour. Many nutritional experts believe oats help to keep cholesterol low.
- ☐ When a recipe requires thinly sliced beef, partially freeze beef first for easy slicing.

EUROPEAN CLASSICS

A selection of delicious, healthy dishes to silence the critics and encourage the cautious. These gastronomic delights are as good for you as they are quick to prepare and satisfying to eat.

CUISINE NATURELLE

The health revolution has finally caught up with the French and, mercifully, it is now possible to delight in French food not swimming in butter, cream, oil, salt, sugar and egg yolks. The low-fat trend has even had an effect on Parisian restaurants where lighter sauces, steamed, baked or poached dishes and crisp salads are now available.

The following recipes belong to a style sometimes called *cuisine naturelle*. They make full use of the wonderful Gallic ability to turn a basic meal of bread, salad, fruit and wine into an occasion.

Bon appetit!

SALAD NICOISE

I spent a wonderful week in Nice where this legendary salad was invented.

3 hard-boiled eggs
1 lettuce
1 bunch endive
3 tomatoes, sliced
150 g (5 oz) green beans, trimmed and lightly steamed
200 g (6½ oz) new potatoes, peeled, steamed and diced
1 green capsicum, thinly sliced
425 g (13½ oz) canned tuna (water-packed variety only)
2 tablespoons chopped fresh parsley

DRESSING
1 cup unsweetened orange juice
2 teaspoons white wine vinegar
1 teaspoon finely chopped fresh basil
1 clove garlic, finely chopped
freshly ground black pepper

Discard egg yolks and slice whites. Arrange salad ingredients in a bowl or on a platter. Mix together dressing ingredients and pour over salad.

Serves 4–6

COUNTRY BEEF TERRINE

2 medium-sized carrots, peeled and chopped
1 medium-sized white onion, chopped
1 medium-sized green capsicum, seeded
2 cloves garlic
1 tablespoon fresh rosemary or 1 teaspoon dried rosemary
500 g (1 lb) lean minced beef, trimmed of any visible fat
freshly ground black pepper
1 tablespoon dry white wine
1 egg white
1 cup homemade Pritikin breadcrumbs
1 tablespoon tomato paste

Finely chop and blend all vegetables, garlic and rosemary. Add to meat with pepper, wine, egg white, breadcrumbs and tomato paste. Mix until well combined.

Spoon into a 28 cm × 10 cm (11 in × 4 in) foil-lined loaf tin. (Non-stick cookware can be very lightly greased with 1–2 drops of olive oil, instead of using foil.)

Bake for 1 hour. Remove from tin and allow to cool. Wrap and refrigerate. Best eaten the next day.

Serves 4–6

Country Beef Terrine and Salad Nicoise

CHICKEN AND PEACH TERRINE

1 kg (2 lb 2 oz) chicken fillets, skinned and trimmed of any visible fat
1 ripe golden peach or 1 cup well drained peaches in natural juice
1 tablespoon fresh herbs (sage, oregano, thyme) or 1 teaspoon dried herbs
1 onion, chopped
1 carrot, peeled and chopped
1 egg white, lightly beaten
squeeze lemon juice
1 cup homemade Pritikin breadcrumbs (see *Note*)
freshly ground black pepper

Preheat oven to 190°C (375°F). Mince chicken in blender, remove and set aside. Peel peach and remove stone. (If using canned variety, dry peaches in a clean tea towel.)

Blend peach, herbs, onion and carrot. Add to chicken mince. Combine with egg white, lemon juice, breadcrumbs and pepper.

Spoon into a 28 cm × 10 cm (11 in × 4 in) foil-lined or non-stick loaf tin. Cookware can be greased with no more than 1–2 drops of olive oil, instead of using foil.) Bake for 1 hour. Remove from tin, cool and wrap. This dish tastes best eaten cold the next day.

Note: Make your own breadcrumbs by placing Pritikin bread in a blender for a few seconds.

Serves 4–6

VEGETABLE TERRINE

3 medium-sized potatoes, peeled and chopped
1 Granny Smith apple, peeled, cored and chopped
1 medium-sized onion, chopped
3 cloves garlic, chopped
1 teaspoon grated Geska cheese
3 medium-sized carrots, peeled and chopped
1 medium-sized red capsicum, seeded
½ fresh red chilli
4 medium-sized zucchini
1 tablespoon chopped fresh parsley
1 teaspoon finely chopped fresh or dried herbs (rosemary, thyme or oregano)
1 cup wholemeal Pritikin breadcrumbs
4 egg whites, lightly beaten
freshly ground black pepper

Blend potatoes, apple, onion, garlic and Geska cheese until finely minced. Set aside. Blend carrots, capsicum and chilli until finely minced and set aside. Blend zucchini, parsley and herbs until finely minced and set aside.

Squeeze as much juice as possible out of the three lots of minced vegetables. Divide breadcrumbs into 3 portions and mix one portion into each vegetable mixture. Mix one egg white only into each vegetable mixture.

Grind pepper over all ingredients and preheat oven to 190°C (375°F).

Line a 28 cm × 10 cm (11 in × 4 in) non-stick loaf tin with foil, or grease with no more than 1–2 drops olive oil. Spoon potato mixture firmly into bottom of tin. Make the next layer with carrot and capsicum mixture. Top with zucchini mixture, and brush with remaining lightly beaten egg white. Bake for 50 minutes.

When cool, carefully unmould. Wrap in foil, refrigerate, and serve cold the following day.

Serves 4–6

BOEUF BOURGUIGNON

1 kg (2 lb 2 oz) topside steak, trimmed of all visible fat and diced
½ cup water
2 large white onions, thinly sliced
1 carrot, peeled and thinly sliced
1 tablespoon wholemeal flour
freshly ground black pepper
2½ cups red wine
1 bay leaf
2 teaspoons tomato paste
2 cloves garlic, finely chopped
1 bouquet garni
150 g (5 oz) mushrooms, washed, stems removed, caps sliced in half
chopped parsley for garnish

Preheat non-stick saucepan. Saute meat for 3–4 minutes and remove from heat. Remove meat from saucepan and set aside.

Add water to saucepan. Bring to the boil and add onions and carrot. Cover and simmer for 3 minutes. Sprinkle over flour and stir until well combined. Add wine, bring to the boil again and allow about one-third to evaporate.

Return meat to saucepan. Add pepper, bay leaf, tomato paste, garlic and bouquet garni. Cover and cook slowly for 2¼ hours.

Add mushrooms and simmer for a further 10 minutes uncovered. Garnish with parsley and serve with boiled potatoes and green beans.

Serves 4–6

COQ AU VIN

1 cup water
2 onions, chopped
2 cloves garlic, finely chopped
1.6 kg (3 lb 2 oz) chicken, skinned and cut into pieces
1 heaped tablespoon wholemeal flour
2 bay leaves
2 carrots, peeled and sliced
2 very ripe tomatoes, chopped
2 teaspoons tomato paste
2 cups red wine
freshly ground black pepper
1 tablespoon chopped fresh parsley
200 g (6½ oz) button mushrooms, wiped clean and halved

Place water in a large saucepan and bring to the boil. Add onions and garlic. Cover and simmer for 5 minutes. Sprinkle chicken pieces with flour and add to saucepan with bay leaves. Reduce heat, cover and simmer for 5 minutes. Add all other ingredients except parsley and mushrooms. Cover and simmer slowly for 35 minutes.

Add mushrooms and simmer for a further 10 minutes. Stir through chopped parsley and serve.

Serves 4–6

TARRAGON CHICKEN

1 white onion
1.6 kg (3 lb 2 oz) chicken, skinned
½ cup defatted chicken stock (see recipe)
2 tablespoons finely chopped fresh tarragon or 2 teaspoons dried tarragon
3 sprigs fresh parsley
freshly ground black pepper

Preheat oven to 200°C (400°F). Place onion inside cavity of chicken. Pour chicken stock over chicken and sprinkle over other ingredients. Place in ovenproof dish and cover with foil. Bake for 15 minutes, then reduce heat to 180°C (350°F) and bake for another hour. Remove foil and cook for a further 15 minutes until chicken is brown. Baste with pan juices during cooking.

Serves 4–6

Boeuf Bourguignon

RIVIERA PAELLA

Although paella is traditionally a Spanish dish you can eat delicious paellas all along the French coast. Small portions of chicken, rabbit and even snails, are sometimes added to French paellas. This recipe is great fun for a dinner party. Use your largest frypan and, if you think you are going to be a regular paella eater, buy a massive Spanish paella pan.

150 g (5 oz) cleaned squid
¾ cup defatted chicken stock (see recipe)
2 cloves garlic, chopped
1 white onion, chopped
4 ripe medium-sized tomatoes, chopped
3 tablespoons tomato paste
2 chicken breasts, trimmed of all visible fat and chopped into small pieces
½ red capsicum, seeded and diced
1 teaspoon paprika
2 pinches saffron threads
freshly ground black pepper
1 kg (2 lb 2 oz) firm fish fillets, cut into chunks
125 g (4 oz) shelled fresh peas
200 g (6½ oz) uncooked (green) prawns, shelled and deveined, tails left on
1½ cups dry white wine
12 uncooked mussels in their shells, trimmed and well scrubbed
6 cups cooked brown rice
lemon wedges, for garnish

Cut squid into rings and cook in boiling water to cover for 5 minutes. Drain and set aside.

Preheat large non-stick frypan and add chicken stock. Bring to the boil and add garlic, onion, tomatoes and tomato paste. Saute in stock for 2–3 minutes.

Add chicken pieces and red capsicum and stir-fry for a further 8 minutes. Add paprika, saffron, pepper, fish pieces and peas. Simmer for 5 minutes.

Top with prawns and wine and continue simmering for a further 3–4 minutes. Add mussels and squid and simmer for another 10 minutes. Discard any mussels which remain tightly closed.

Carefully remove everything from the pan. Place cooked brown rice in pan and heat through with small amount of pan juices. Return paella mixture to pan on top of rice. Simmer for a further 2–3 minutes. Add a little extra water or dash of wine if necessary.

Serve garnished with lemon wedges. It is usual to bring the paella pan to the table for people to help themselves.

Serves 4–6

STEAK WITH PEPPER SAUCE

4 small steaks (fillet or rump), trimmed of all visible fat
½ cup dry sherry
finely chopped fresh parsley for garnish
SAUCE
1¼ cups defatted beef or chicken stock (see recipe)
1 tablespoon finely chopped white onion
2 tablespoons cornflour
2 teaspoons freshly ground black pepper
1 teaspoon brandy
pinch hot paprika

Marinate steak in sherry for at least 2 hours. To make sauce, bring ½ cup stock to the boil. Add onion, cover and simmer for 3 minutes. Mix cornflour with remaining stock. Add to saucepan with pepper, brandy and sherry marinade. Simmer and stir for 2–3 minutes. Stir in paprika. Set aside and keep warm.

Grill steaks until tender (5–10 minutes each side, depending on thickness). Pour over sauce, garnish with parsley and serve.

Serves 4–6

STOCKS

Stocks are fundamental to good French and other cuisines, and necessary for many soups and sauces. These three are quick and easy to make. For a more concentrated flavour, remove cover and reduce liquid by boiling.

VEGETABLE STOCK

8 cups water
2 carrots, sliced
2 large white onions, sliced
3 stalks celery with leaves, chopped
2 cloves garlic, chopped
3 sprigs fresh parsley, chopped
1 sprig fresh thyme
1 bay leaf

Place all ingredients in a large saucepan and bring to the boil. Reduce heat, cover and simmer for 1 hour. Strain liquid through a fine sieve. Store in refrigerator and reserve for soups and sauces.

Makes approximately 7 cups

FISH STOCK

1 kg (2 lb 2 oz) mixed fish bones (include some flesh, heads and trimmings; add a few uncooked prawns and calamari rings)
2 cleaned and trimmed mussels
1 large white onion, thinly sliced
1 stalk celery with leaves, sliced
1 cup dry white wine
6 black peppercorns
1 sprig fresh thyme
2 sprigs fresh parsley
8 cups water
juice 1 lemon

Place all ingredients in a large saucepan and bring to the boil. Reduce heat, cover and simmer for 20 minutes. Skim the surface and strain through a fine sieve. Store in refrigerator and use as required.

Makes approximately 8 cups

CHICKEN OR BEEF STOCK

1 kg (2 lb 2 oz) skinned chicken pieces and bones or beef, trimmed of all visible fat
1 large white onion, sliced
1 carrot, sliced
1 stalk celery with leaves, chopped
1 bay leaf
3 sprigs fresh parsley, chopped
4 peppercorns
8 cups water

Place all ingredients in a large saucepan and bring to the boil. Reduce heat, cover and simmer for 1½ hours. Strain the stock through a fine sieve and allow to cool. Refrigerate overnight, and in the morning skim off the surface fat.

Makes approximately 7 cups

Riviera Paella

FRENCH ONION SOUP

7 cups defatted beef or vegetable stock (see recipe)
4 medium-sized white onions, finely sliced
1 clove garlic, chopped
1 tablespoon wholemeal flour
½ cup dry white wine
1 bay leaf
freshly ground black pepper
2 teaspoons finely chopped fresh parsley

CHEESE CROUTONS
1 cup fresh ricotta or low-fat cottage cheese
1 teaspoon grated Geska cheese
freshly ground black pepper
4 slices Pritikin thick sliced bread

Bring 2 cups stock to the boil. Add onions and garlic, cover and simmer for 20 minutes. Sprinkle over wholemeal flour. Stir and cook for a further 2 minutes. Add remaining stock with wine, bay leaf and pepper. Bring to the boil, cover and simmer slowly for 40 minutes. Occasionally skim surface.

To make croutons, preheat oven to 190°C (375°F). Mash cheeses with pepper and spread onto toast slices. Cut into small squares or round shapes, and bake for 20 minutes. To serve, ladle out soup and top with croutons and chopped parsley.

Serves 4–6

PARISIAN FISH SOUP

8 cups fish stock (see recipe)
½ cup white wine
300 g (10 oz) very ripe tomatoes, seeded and diced
1 clove garlic, chopped
1 teaspoon orange zest, grated
½ fresh red chilli, finely chopped
3 sprigs fresh parsley, chopped
1 sprig fresh thyme
1–2 saffron threads
750 g (1½ lb) fish fillets, cut into large chunks
250 g (8 oz) green (uncooked) prawns, shelled and deveined
10 mussels, thoroughly cleaned
extra chopped fresh parsley, for garnish

Place stock, wine, tomatoes, garlic, orange zest, chilli, parsley, thyme and saffron in a large saucepan. Bring to the boil. Reduce heat, cover and simmer for 20 minutes. Strain through a fine sieve.

Bring liquid to the boil again and add fish chunks. Reduce heat, cover and simmer for 5 minutes. Add prawns and mussels and simmer for a further 5 minutes. Discard any mussels that don't open. Garnish with parsley and serve with wholemeal Pritikin bread.

Serves 4–6

VICHYSSOISE

4 cups defatted chicken stock (see recipe)
1 white onion, sliced
4 leeks, white part only, chopped and well washed
1 tablespoon chopped fresh parsley
1 stalk celery and 2 leaves, chopped
3 medium-sized potatoes, peeled and finely sliced
freshly ground black pepper
½ cup skim milk

Bring ½ cup stock to the boil and add onion and leeks. Cover and simmer for 5 minutes. Add remaining stock, parsley, celery, potatoes and pepper and simmer for 20 minutes.

Cool, then puree and stir in skim milk. Chill and serve.

Serves 4–6

SALMON MOUSSE

420 g (14 oz) canned red salmon, well drained
1 tablespoon white wine vinegar
1 tablespoon gelatine
¼ cup water
125 g (4 oz) ricotta cheese combined with 1 tablespoon skim milk
2 teaspoons tomato paste
½ cup finely chopped celery
4 shallots, finely chopped
1 tablespoon cucumber, peeled, seeded and finely chopped
2 teaspoons chopped fresh dill
1 teaspoon cayenne pepper
freshly ground black pepper

Blend salmon with vinegar until smooth. Mix gelatine with water and dissolve. Stir ricotta and milk mixture into gelatine and water. Stir into blended salmon.

Add tomato paste, celery, shallots, cucumber, dill and peppers. Mix until well combined.

Pour into a glass mould or dish. Cover and chill overnight. Unmould carefully and serve with crudites (see recipe).

Serves 4–6

French Onion Soup

LEEKS VINAIGRETTE

4 leeks, ends trimmed and sliced in
    half lengthways
1 cup water
DRESSING
1 teaspoon red wine vinegar
½ cup fresh orange juice
2 shallots, very finely chopped
1 clove garlic, minced
1 tablespoon chopped fresh parsley
freshly ground black pepper

Place leeks in saucepan with water.
Cover and simmer for 15 minutes. Drain,
cool and place on serving dish. Combine
dressing ingredients, pour over leeks and
serve.

Serves 4–6

CRUDITES

2 stalks celery, sliced diagonally
4 carrots, peeled and sliced
100 g (3½ oz) cauliflower, separated
    into florets
8 radishes, trimmed
1 red capsicum, seeded and sliced in
    thin strips
1 green capsicum, seeded and sliced
    in thin strips
4 shallots, trimmed and cut into short
    lengths
100 g (3½ oz) butternut pumpkin, cut
    into curls with potato peeler
100 g (3½ oz) zucchini, trimmed and
    sliced
alfalfa sprouts, for garnish

Arrange the vegetables attractively,
garnish with alfalfa sprouts and serve with
your favourite dressing.

Serves 4–6

BEETROOT AND
SHALLOT SALAD

6 fresh medium-sized beetroot
4 shallots, diced
½ cup fresh orange juice
1 teaspoon red wine vinegar
1 tablespoon chopped chives
freshly ground black pepper

Steam the beetroot until tender, peel and
dice. Combine all ingredients, chill and
serve.

Serves 4–6

RATATOUILLE

1 medium-sized eggplant, thickly
    diced
2 white onions, finely sliced
2 cloves garlic, finely chopped
2 medium-sized zucchini, sliced
2 very ripe medium-sized tomatoes,
    sliced
1 tablespoon tomato paste, mixed
    with 1 cup water
freshly ground black pepper
1 red capsicum, seeded and sliced
2 sprigs fresh parsley
1 sprig fresh thyme

Place diced eggplant on kitchen paper
for 20 minutes to absorb bitter juices.
Rinse and pat dry.
    Combine all ingredients except parsley
and thyme. Bring to the boil, reduce heat
and simmer for 15 minutes. Add parsley
and thyme and simmer for a further 5
minutes. Serve with wholemeal bread.

Serves 4–6

OAT CREPES WITH
PEACH PUREE

425 g (13½ oz) canned peaches in
    natural juice
3 cups raw oats, blended to a fine
    flour
dash mixed spice
1 egg white, well beaten
2 cups skim milk
low-fat yoghurt, for garnish

Drain off half peach juice and puree fruit.
Combine oat flour thoroughly with mixed
spice, egg white and milk.
    Preheat a non-stick frypan to very hot.
Ladle out a dollop of oat mixture and
rotate pan until crepe spreads into a
circle. Cook until bubbles appear, then
turn over with non-stick spatula and cook
other side.
    Serve each person a stack of 2–3
crepes. Pour over peach puree and
serve with a spoonful of yoghurt on top.
Also delicious sprinkled with a few drops
of your favourite liqueur.

Serves 4–6

GREEN BEANS AND
MUSHROOMS

1 kg (2 lb 2 oz) green beans, trimmed
250 g (8 oz) button mushrooms
SAUCE
1 cup low-fat yoghurt
¼ cup chopped chives
freshly ground black pepper

Steam beans for 5–10 minutes until
tender. Place mushrooms on top of
beans, steam for a further 2 minutes, then
arrange on a serving plate. Mix together
sauce ingredients, pour over vegetables.

Serves 4–6

BRAISED RED AND
WHITE CABBAGE

1½ cups vegetable or defatted
    chicken stock (see recipe)
1 large white onion, finely sliced
¼ small red cabbage, cored and
    coarsely shredded
¼ small green cabbage, cored and
    coarsely shredded
1 teaspoon caraway seeds
¼ cup fresh lemon juice
freshly ground black pepper
1 tablespoon chopped fresh parsley

Place stock in a saucepan and bring to
the boil. Add onion, cover and simmer for
5 minutes. Add red and green cabbage,
cover and simmer over low heat for 30
minutes. Add caraway seeds, lemon juice
and pepper. Cover and simmer for a
further 5 minutes. Sprinkle with parsley.

Serves 4–6

SALMON RICE SALAD
WITH PERNOD

3 hard-boiled eggs
210 g (7 oz) water-packed canned
    salmon
1 head fennel, thinly sliced
½ cup low-fat yoghurt
2 shallots, finely sliced
3 cups cooked brown rice
1 teaspoon chopped fresh dill
squeeze lemon juice
1 teaspoon Pernod
freshly ground black pepper

Discard egg yolks and chop whites only.
Combine all ingredients, chill and serve.

Serves 4–6

Gero cutlery

LA CUCINA SENSAZIONALE

Not all Italian food contains olive oil, Parmesan cheese, olives, butter and cream. Pasta, pizza, risotto, minestrone, gelato and many other irresistible Italian treats can be prepared using low-fat, low-cholesterol ingredients.

Garlic, basil, thyme, oregano and rosemary are the essence of authentic Italian cooking — grow your own if at all possible and always select the freshest lean meat, seafood, chicken, vegetables and fruit.

Many Italian cheeses do have too much fat and salt to be included in Pritikin-style recipes, so use ricotta and cottage cheeses as a good alternative.

Buon appetito!

EASY PIZZA DOUGH

3½ cups wholemeal self-raising flour
125 g (4 oz) fresh ricotta cheese
1⅓ cups skim milk

Sift the flour. Tip bran husks back into the bowl. Rub in the ricotta cheese until the mixture resembles breadcrumbs. Slowly add the skim milk until a soft dough is formed.

Place dough on floured board and knead for 5 minutes until smooth and elastic. Allow to stand for 1 hour wrapped in a clean tea towel. Using a lightly floured rolling pin, roll out to between 0.5–1 cm (¼–½ inch) thick.

To cut out a round pizza, place a dinner plate on the rolled out dough and slice round the edge with a sharp knife. For mini pizzas, cut round the rim of a drinking glass. Place pizza base on a pizza or non-stick baking tray.

Preheat oven to 200°C (400°F). Add topping of your choice and bake for 25 minutes. Serve hot or cold.
Note: If you are in a hurry, wholemeal pita bread can serve as a pizza base.

Makes 1 large pizza, 2 medium-sized or 6 mini pizzas

Pizza with Vegetarian Supreme Pizza Topping, and Spinach and Ricotta Topping

BASIC PIZZA TOMATO SAUCE

1 medium-sized onion
2 cloves garlic
4 very ripe medium-sized tomatoes
1 tablespoon tomato paste
1 tablespoon finely chopped fresh oregano or 1 teaspoon dried oregano
1 tablespoon finely chopped fresh basil or 1 teaspoon dried basil
¼ cup water
1 teaspoon red wine vinegar
freshly ground black pepper

Blend all the ingredients together.

Sufficient for 1 pizza

VEGETARIAN SUPREME PIZZA TOPPING

1 quantity basic pizza tomato sauce (see recipe)
1 red or green capsicum, cut in thin strips
1 cup finely sliced button mushrooms, cleaned and sliced
1 zucchini, finely sliced
1 cup fresh ricotta cheese
1 tablespoon chopped fresh parsley

Spread uncooked pizza base with tomato sauce. Add vegetables. Sprinkle with cheese and parsley and bake at 200°C (400°F) for 25 minutes.

Sufficient for 1 pizza

SPINACH AND RICOTTA TOPPING

250 g (8 oz) fresh ricotta cheese
1 tablespoon skim milk
2 cups finely chopped fresh uncooked spinach
1 tablespoon finely chopped fresh parsley
½ teaspoon freshly grated nutmeg

Puree ricotta cheese with skim milk. Mix in chopped spinach and parsley. Spread onto uncooked pizza base. Sprinkle with nutmeg and bake at 200°C (400°F) for 25 minutes.

Sufficient for 1 pizza

MINESTRONE SOUP

2 medium-sized onions, finely sliced
2 cloves garlic, finely chopped
4 cups defatted chicken, beef or
  vegetable stock (see recipe)
1 cup finely chopped celery
3 carrots, peeled and finely sliced
2 zucchini, finely chopped
3 very ripe tomatoes, finely chopped
3 tablespoons tomato paste
3 cups cooked dried beans (borlotti
  or cannellini)
2 tablespoons finely chopped fresh
  oregano or 2 teaspoons dried
  oregano
1 cup cooked brown rice
freshly ground black pepper

Place onions and garlic in a large
saucepan with 2 cups stock. Simmer
covered for 5 minutes. Add all other
ingredients to saucepan except fresh
herbs, rice and pepper. Simmer covered
for 30 minutes.

Puree half the soup and return it to the
saucepan. Add herbs, rice and pepper,
and simmer for 8 minutes. Serve hot with
wholemeal Pritikin bread.

Serves 4–6

ZUCCHINI SOUP

2 medium-sized onions, finely sliced
1 clove garlic, finely chopped
3 cups defatted chicken, beef or
  vegetable stock (see recipe)
3 medium-sized potatoes, peeled and
  diced
½ cup diced celery
750 g (1½ lb) zucchini, roughly
  chopped
1 cup skim milk
1 tablespoon finely chopped fresh
  rosemary or 1 teaspoon dried
  rosemary
freshly ground black pepper

Place onions and garlic in a large
saucepan with 2 cups stock. Simmer
covered for 5 minutes. Add all other
ingredients except rosemary and pepper.
Simmer for 30 minutes. Puree half the
soup and return it to the saucepan. Add
rosemary and pepper and simmer for 5
minutes.

Serves 4–6

Minestrone Soup

PAVAROTTI POTATO AND ONION SOUP

5 medium-sized onions, finely sliced
2 cloves garlic, finely chopped
4 cups defatted chicken, beef or
  vegetable stock (see recipe)
8 medium-sized potatoes, peeled and
  roughly chopped
1 cup skim milk
freshly ground black pepper
finely chopped fresh parsley, for
  garnish

Place onions and garlic in a large
saucepan with 2 cups stock. Simmer
covered for 5 minutes. Add all remaining
ingredients and simmer for 30 minutes.
Puree and serve, garnished with parsley.

Serves 4–6

SPINACH SOUP

1 bunch fresh spinach, with stalks
  removed
2 cloves garlic, chopped
1 medium-sized onion, finely sliced
3 cups defatted chicken, beef or
  vegetable stock (see recipe)
1½ cups skim milk
½ cup chopped fresh parsley
1 teaspoon freshly grated nutmeg
freshly ground black pepper

Wash and finely chop spinach. Place
garlic and onion in a large saucepan with
2 cups stock. Simmer covered for 5
minutes. Add all other ingredients except
nutmeg and pepper. Simmer for 20
minutes. Puree half the soup and return
it to the saucepan. Stir in nutmeg and
pepper. Simmer for 5 minutes and serve.

Serves 4–6

AUSSIE PIZZA TOPPING

1 quantity basic pizza tomato sauce
  (see recipe)
2 cups cooked lean minced beef
5 egg whites, cooked and chopped
1 medium-sized onion, finely
  chopped
2 tablespoons finely chopped fresh
  parsley

Spread tomato sauce onto uncooked
pizza base. Sprinkle with minced beef,
egg whites and onion. Top with parsley
and bake at 200°C (400°F) 25 minutes.
Sufficient for 1 pizza

Sarki Colourstone Grey plate

Siesta Seafood Salad

SIESTA SEAFOOD SALAD

**225 g (7 oz) calamari, washed and
   cleaned**
**225 g (7 oz) scallops, washed and
   trimmed**
225 g (7 oz) fresh cooked prawns
¼ cup red or white wine vinegar
**3 medium-sized carrots, peeled and
   thinly sliced**
**2 medium-sized red onions, finely
   sliced**
**1 red capsicum, seeded and thinly
   sliced**
2 cloves garlic, finely sliced
**1 teaspoon chopped fresh sage or
   ½ teaspoon dried sage**
½ cup fresh lemon juice
freshly ground black pepper
**finely chopped fresh parsley, for
   garnish**

Cut calamari into 5 mm (¼ in) rings. Bring
a large saucepan of water to the boil and
plunge in the calamari. Reduce heat and
simmer for 10 minutes. Drain and put
aside. Re-boil water and plunge in
scallops. Simmer for 5 minutes, and
drain.

Allow seafood to cool, then combine
well with remaining ingredients. Marinate
for 1 hour in refrigerator, garnish with
parsley and serve.

Serves 4–6

TEMPTING TUNA SALAD

**150 g (5 oz) canned cannellini or
   borlotti beans**
**425 g (13½ oz) canned tuna (water-
   packed)**
**1 medium-sized red onion, thinly
   sliced**
¼ cup red wine vinegar
**1 tablespoon finely chopped fresh
   parsley**
squeeze lemon juice
freshly ground black pepper

Rinse beans in cold water to remove
excess salt, and drain. Combine all
ingredients and serve.

Serves 4–6

FENNEL SALAD

2 large fennel bulbs
1 cucumber, finely sliced
1 red capsicum, seeded and sliced
1 small onion, finely sliced
DRESSING
1 cup fresh orange juice
1 teaspoon red or white wine vinegar
1 tablespoon chopped fresh mint
freshly ground black pepper

Remove outer leaves from fennel bulbs
and slice the bulbs finely. Mix with other
salad vegetables. Combine dressing
ingredients and leave in refrigerator for
30 minutes. Pour over salad just before
serving.

Serves 4–6

MIXED ITALIAN SALAD

2 crisp mignonette lettuce
1 radicchio
1 green capsicum, finely sliced
1 red capsicum, finely sliced
2 medium-sized tomatoes, sliced
½ cucumber, finely sliced
1 clove garlic, finely chopped
8 radishes, finely sliced

DRESSING
1 cup fresh orange juice
squeeze fresh lemon juice
**2 teaspoons red or white wine
   vinegar**
**1 tablespoon finely chopped fresh
   parsley**
freshly ground black pepper

Rinse, drain and tear up lettuce leaves
and radicchio. Add all other ingredients
in a bowl. Combine dressing ingredients
and marinate in refrigerator for 30
minutes. Pour over salad just before
serving.

Serves 4–6

CHICKEN CACCIATORE

1.5 kg (3 lb) chicken, skinned, trimmed of all visible fat and cut into 6 pieces
1 medium-sized onion, finely sliced
3 cloves garlic, finely chopped
1½ cups dry white wine
4 very ripe medium-sized tomatoes, roughly chopped
1 tablespoon tomato paste
1 bay leaf
freshly ground black pepper
finely chopped fresh parsley, for garnish

Place all ingredients except parsley in a large saucepan. Cover and simmer for 40 minutes until tender. The gravy can be thickened with 2 teaspoons wholemeal flour mixed with cold water and added to the pan. Remove bay leaf, garnish with parsley and serve.

Serves 4–6

Chicken Cacciatore

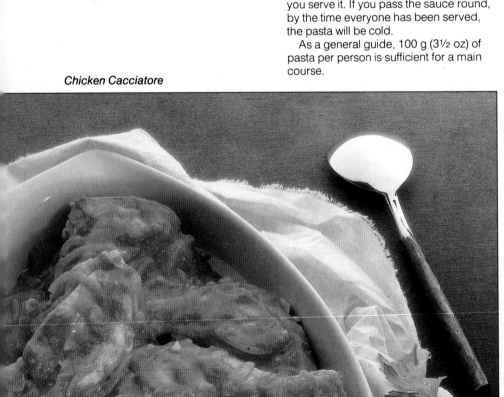

HOW TO COOK AND SERVE PASTA

It is important to use a large saucepan or soup pot. For 1 kg (2 lb 2 oz) of pasta I recommend a minimum of 4 litres (7 pints) of water.

Wait until the water is boiling furiously, then drop in the pasta. If you are using long strands of pasta — spaghetti, fettucine, tagliatelle — bend the pasta into the water. Don't break it up.

It is hard to estimate exactly how long to cook pasta. You **must** test it yourself to see when it is *al dente* — firm to the bite.

Fresh pasta cooks quickly: 2–4 minutes; dried pasta takes 10–12 minutes; and filled pasta — such as ravioli or tortellini — 10 minutes.

There is a strange rumour going round that cooked pasta should immediately be deluged with cold water and drained. Never do that — unless you like gluggy pasta!

When I was a child my mother always spooned the Bolognese sauce on top of our spaghetti. I think it is much better to mix the sauce in with the pasta before you serve it. If you pass the sauce round, by the time everyone has been served, the pasta will be cold.

As a general guide, 100 g (3½ oz) of pasta per person is sufficient for a main course.

PASTA SAUCES

TOMATO SAUCE

1 medium-sized onion, finely sliced
3 cloves garlic, finely chopped
1 cup water
500 g (1 lb) fresh ripe tomatoes, roughly chopped
1 tablespoon tomato paste
freshly ground black pepper

Place onion, garlic and water in a saucepan. Cover and simmer for 5 minutes. Add all other ingredients, cover and simmer for 10 minutes. Puree and serve with freshly cooked pasta.

Alternatively, you can blend the above ingredients, heat through and serve if you want an 'instant' sauce.

Serves 4

TOMATO AND BASIL SAUCE

1 medium-sized onion, finely sliced
3 cloves garlic
1 cup water
500 g (1 lb) very ripe tomatoes
freshly ground black pepper
1 bunch fresh basil, roughly chopped, with stalks removed

Place onion, garlic and water in a saucepan. Cover and simmer for 5 minutes. Add tomatoes and pepper, cover and simmer for 10 minutes. Puree, stir in basil and serve.

Serves 4

CHILLI SAUCE

500 g (1 lb) very ripe tomatoes
1 medium-sized onion, finely chopped
1 tablespoon tomato paste
2 fresh red or green chillies, chopped
½ cup water
freshly ground black pepper

Place all ingredients in a saucepan and simmer covered for 10 minutes. Puree, and serve with freshly cooked pasta.

Serves 4

GARLIC AND PARSLEY SAUCE

Only true garlic lovers will appreciate this addictive sauce.

10 cloves garlic, finely chopped
1 cup finely chopped fresh parsley
1 cup unsweetened orange juice
squeeze lemon juice
freshly ground black pepper

Blend all ingredients and mix through freshly cooked pasta.

Serves 4

Pasta with Tomato and Basil Sauce

TOMATO AND LEMON SAUCE

1 cup fresh lemon juice
500 g (1 lb) very ripe tomatoes
1 tablespoon tomato paste
1 clove garlic
freshly ground black pepper

Place all ingredients in a saucepan and simmer covered for 10 minutes. Puree, simmer for a further 5 minutes and serve with freshly cooked pasta.

Serves 4

MUSHROOM AND RICOTTA SAUCE

300 g (9½ oz) fresh ricotta cheese
1 cup skim milk
2 cloves garlic, finely chopped
freshly ground black pepper
300 g (9½ oz) fresh button mushrooms, cleaned and sliced
finely chopped fresh parsley, for garnish

Puree ricotta cheese with skim milk, garlic and black pepper. Stir in sliced mushrooms. Garnish with parsley.

Serves 4

HEY PESTO SAUCE

I think this sauce is the *pesto de resistance*! It is light, zesty and 'different'.

1 large bunch fresh basil, with stalks removed (dried basil is not an option if you want the real thing)
6 cloves garlic
½ cup pine nuts (optional)
300 g (9½ oz) fresh ricotta cheese
¾ cup skim milk
freshly ground black pepper

Mash all ingredients in a mortar and pestle, or blend together. Mix through freshly cooked pasta.

Serves 4

BOLOGNESE SAUCE

400 g (13 oz) lean minced beef
1 cup water
1 clove garlic, finely chopped
1 medium-sized onion, finely sliced
1 tablespoon tomato paste
1 cup diced celery
1 medium-sized carrot, peeled and diced
1 tablespoon chopped fresh oregano or 1 teaspoon dried oregano
1½ cups dry white wine
3 ripe medium-sized tomatoes, roughly chopped
freshly ground black pepper

Place beef, water, garlic and onion in a non-stick frypan. Cover and simmer for 5 minutes. Add the remaining ingredients and simmer covered for 30 minutes. Serve with freshly cooked pasta.

Serves 4

TUNA AND CELERY SAUCE

1 cup water
1 medium-sized red onion, finely
    sliced
1 clove garlic, finely chopped
425 g (13½ oz) canned tuna (water-
    packed)
3 very ripe medium-sized tomatoes,
    roughly chopped
1 teaspoon finely chopped fresh sage
    or ½ teaspoon dried sage
2 cups diced celery, including 1–2
    leaves, chopped
2 tablespoons finely chopped fresh
    parsley

Place water, onion and garlic in non-stick
frypan. Simmer covered for 5 minutes.
Add all other ingredients and simmer for
5 minutes. This sauce is also delicious
served cold with cold pasta.

Serves 4

MUSHROOMS WITH GARLIC

500 g (1 lb) button mushrooms, wiped
    clean and thinly sliced
3 cloves garlic, finely chopped
1 red onion, finely chopped
2 tablespoons white wine vinegar
2 tablespoons fresh orange juice
2 tablespoons finely chopped
    parsley, for garnish

Combine all ingredients and allow to
stand for 1 hour. Serve as a cold entree
or appetiser.

Serves 4–6

TUSCAN TOMATOES

8 medium-sized tomatoes, sliced
1 tablespoon finely chopped fresh
    oregano or 1 teaspoon dried
    oregano
1 clove garlic, finely chopped
1 cup unsweetened orange juice
1 teaspoon red wine vinegar
freshly ground black pepper

Mix all ingredients together, chill and
serve as a cold entree or appetiser.

Serves 4–6

HERBED POTATO CROQUETTES

1 kg (2 lb 2 oz) potatoes, peeled,
    boiled and mashed
2 cloves garlic, finely chopped
100 g (3½ oz) fresh ricotta cheese
2 teaspoons grated Geska cheese
1 tablespoon finely chopped fresh
    oregano or 1 teaspoon dried
    oregano
1 tablespoon finely chopped fresh
    basil or 1 teaspoon dried basil
freshly ground black pepper
3 egg whites, lightly beaten
2 cups homemade wholemeal Pritikin
    breadcrumbs

Preheat oven to 200°C (400°F). Combine
mashed potato, garlic, ricotta and Geska
cheese, herbs and pepper. Roll mixture
into small balls. Dip into egg whites and
coat firmly with breadcrumbs. Bake for
30 minutes until brown.

Serves 4–6

STUFFED TOMATOES

8 very ripe medium-sized tomatoes
1 medium-sized onion, finely
    chopped
1 clove garlic, finely chopped
¼ cup water
½ green or red capsicum, seeded and
    finely chopped
2 cups cooked brown rice
1 tablespoon finely chopped fresh
    basil or 1 teaspoon dried basil
1 tablespoon finely chopped fresh
    parsley
250 g (8 oz) fresh ricotta cheese
1 teaspoon grated Geska cheese

Preheat oven to 180°C (350°F). Slice the
top off each tomato and set aside the
tops. Scoop out tomato flesh and chop.
Reserve tomato cases.
    Simmer onion and garlic in water for 5
minutes. Combine all remaining
ingredients and mix well. Drain off excess
liquid and spoon mixture into tomato
cases. Put tomato tops back and place
on non-stick baking tray. Bake for 15
minutes and serve.

Serves 4–6

SPINACH LASAGNE

1 bay leaf
1 large bunch fresh spinach, with
    stalks removed
250 g (8 oz) spinach or wholemeal
    lasagne sheets (about 12)
500 g (1 lb) fresh ricotta cheese
1 tablespoon grated Geska cheese
2½ cups wholemeal Pritikin
    breadcrumbs
4 very ripe medium-sized tomatoes,
    finely sliced
1 medium-sized onion, finely
    chopped
2 cloves garlic, finely chopped
1 tablespoon finely chopped fresh
    basil or 1 teaspoon dried basil
1 tablespoon finely chopped fresh
    oregano or 1 teaspoon dried
    oregano
2 tablespoons tomato paste, mixed
    with 1½ cups water or vegetable
    stock
freshly ground black pepper
1 teaspoon freshly grated nutmeg

Place bay leaf in a large saucepan of
water and bring to the boil. Drop in
spinach leaves for 1 minute. Remove,
drain well, chop finely and set aside.
    Bring a large saucepan of water to the
boil. Drop in lasagne sheets, three at a
time. Cook for 10–12 minutes until
tender. Plunge into cold water, drain and
set aside. (The pre-cooked lasagne
sheets do not need to be boiled.)
    Mix ricotta and Geska cheese with
breadcrumbs until mixture is crumbly,
and divide into 4 portions.
    Preheat oven to 200°C (400°F). Layer
a 30 cm × 20 cm (12 in × 8 in) non-stick
baking dish in the following order:
• 4 lasagne sheets
• portion of ricotta, Geska and
    breadcrumb mixture
• spinach
• tomatoes
• onion and garlic
• basil and oregano.
    Repeat the process three times and
top with a layer of lasagne sheets. Pour
over tomato paste and water mixture.
Sprinkle with remaining ricotta, Geska
and breadcrumb mixture. Season with
pepper and sprinkle with nutmeg. Bake
for 40 minutes until top is brown.

Serves 4–6

STUFFED ZUCCHINI

8 medium-sized zucchini
1 cup homemade wholemeal Pritikin
    breadcrumbs
1 tablespoon finely chopped fresh
    oregano or 1 teaspoon dried
    oregano
1 clove garlic, finely chopped
1 small onion, finely chopped
freshly ground black pepper
250 g (8 oz) fresh ricotta cheese

Preheat oven to 200°C (400°F). Bring a
large saucepan of water to the boil.
Plunge zucchini in for 2 minutes and
drain in colander. Cut in half lengthways
and scoop out flesh. Set aside.

Mix breadcrumbs, oregano, garlic,
onion, pepper and ricotta cheese until
mixture is crumbly. Mix in zucchini flesh.
Stuff mixture back into zucchini shells
and bake for 20 minutes.

Serves 4–6

EGGPLANT AND TOMATO BAKE

1 kg (2 lb 2 oz) medium-sized
    eggplants, thinly sliced
4 very ripe medium-sized tomatoes,
    sliced
2 tablespoons finely chopped fresh
    oregano or 2 teaspoons dried
    oregano
1 tablespoon finely chopped fresh
    parsley
1 tablespoon tomato paste
1 cup dry white wine
300 g (9½ oz) fresh ricotta cheese
1 teaspoon grated Geska cheese
1½ cups wholemeal Pritikin
    breadcrumbs
freshly ground black pepper

Preheat oven to 200°C (400°F). Place
eggplant slices on kitchen paper for 20
minutes. Rinse and pat dry. Layer
alternately with tomato slices in medium-
sized ovenproof dish. Sprinkle with
oregano and parsley. Mix tomato paste
with white wine and pour over. Combine
ricotta and Geska cheese with breadcrumbs and spoon on top. Sprinkle with
pepper and bake for 40 minutes until
brown on top.

Serves 4–6

BEEF IN RED WINE

600 g (1¼ lb) lean beef, trimmed of all
    visible fat and diced
250 g (8 oz) button mushrooms, finely
    sliced
1 medium-sized onion, finely sliced
2 tablespoons tomato paste
1 bay leaf
3 medium-sized zucchini, finely
    sliced
2 cloves garlic, finely chopped
1½ cups red wine
1½ cups water
1 teaspoon finely chopped fresh
    marjoram or ½ teaspoon dried
    marjoram
freshly ground black pepper
1 tablespoon wholemeal flour, mixed
    with 2 tablespoons cold water

Place diced beef in a non-stick frypan
and saute for 5 minutes. Put all
ingredients except flour into a large
saucepan. Cover and simmer for 1 hour.
Stir in flour and water mixture, and
simmer for 5 minutes. Remove bay leaf
and serve.

Serves 4–6

BEEF BIANCO

½ cup skim milk
250 g (8 oz) fresh ricotta cheese
6 small beefsteaks, trimmed of all
    visible fat
1 medium-sized onion, thinly sliced
1 clove garlic, finely chopped
¼ cup water
1 cup dry sherry or white wine
1 tablespoon wholemeal flour mixed
    with 2 tablespoons cold water
125 g (4 oz) button mushrooms, thinly
    sliced
freshly ground black pepper

Puree skim milk with ricotta cheese and
set aside. Flatten beefsteaks until thin.

In non-stick frypan, cover and simmer
onion and garlic in water for 5 minutes.
Add beef and cook for 2 minutes on each
side. Add sherry, flour and water mixture,
mushrooms and pepper. Simmer, stirring
for 4 minutes.

Pour in ricotta cheese and skim milk
puree. Heat through without allowing it to
boil, and serve.

Serves 4–6

PEASANT CHICKEN CASSEROLE

1.5 kg (3 lb) chicken, skinned,
    trimmed of all visible fat and cut
    into 6 pieces
4 cups defatted chicken or vegetable
    stock (see recipe)
2 medium-sized onions, finely sliced
2 cloves garlic, finely chopped
250 g (8 oz) button mushrooms,
    sliced
1 bay leaf
2 sprigs fresh thyme
1 tablespoon cornflour
freshly ground black pepper
finely chopped fresh parsley, for
    garnish

Place all ingredients except parsley in a
large saucepan. Cover and simmer for
40 minutes. Remove bay leaf, garnish
with parsley and serve.

Serves 4–6

FISH FEAST

1 kg (2 lb 2 oz) assorted, uncooked,
    cleaned fish (include a few
    uncooked [green] prawns and
    calamari pieces)
1 bay leaf
2 cups dry white wine
2 medium-sized onions, roughly
    chopped
1 tablespoon tomato paste
3 very ripe medium-sized tomatoes,
    roughly chopped
freshly ground black pepper
1 tablespoon finely chopped fresh
    parsley

Cut fish into small chunks; roughly slice
prawns and calamari. Combine all
ingredients except parsley in a
saucepan. Cover and simmer on low
heat for 25 minutes. Remove bay leaf,
sprinkle with parsley and serve.

Serves 4–6

GENOA GRILLED FISH

1 whole fish (snapper, whiting, perch), cleaned and scaled
lemon wedges, for garnish

MARINADE
1 cup lemon juice
1 tablespoon white wine vinegar
1 clove garlic, finely chopped
1 tablespoon chopped fresh rosemary or 1 teaspoon dried rosemary
2 bay leaves

Combine marinade ingredients and marinate fish in the mixture for 2 hours. Preheat griller to high. Grill fish for 5 minutes on each side, or until flesh is white when flaked with a fork. Garnish with lemon wedges and serve.

Serves 4–6

GARLIC PRAWNS

500 g (1 lb) fresh uncooked (green) prawns, shelled and deveined
lemon wedges, for garnish

MARINADE
6 cloves garlic, finely chopped
1 tablespoon finely chopped fresh parsley
¼ cup fresh lemon juice
freshly ground black pepper

Combine marinade ingredients and marinate prawns for 1 hour. Drain off lemon juice, making sure prawns are still coated with garlic and parsley. Preheat griller to high and grill prawns for 3 minutes on each side. Garnish with lemon wedges and serve.

Serves 4–6

FIGARO CAKE

4 egg whites
1½ cups wholemeal self-raising flour, sifted
400 g (12½ oz) dried figs, finely chopped
zest 1 orange, grated
zest 1 lemon, grated
1 cup finely chopped pine nuts
1 teaspoon freshly grated nutmeg

Preheat oven to 200°C (400°F). Beat egg whites until stiff, combine gently with all ingredients and mix thoroughly. Bake in a 28 cm × 10 cm (11 in × 4 in) non-stick loaf tin for 35 minutes. Allow cake to cook in tin. Remove, wrap in foil and refrigerate for 24 hours before cutting.

Serves 4–6

Garlic Prawns

PEACH GELATO

4 fresh golden peaches
2 cups fresh orange juice
¼ cup fresh lemon juice
1 tablespoon gelatine mixed with
 2 tablespoons hot water
fresh mint, for garnish

Peel peaches, remove stones and puree
the flesh. Add orange and lemon juices
and stir in gelatine. Pour into ice-cream
trays and freeze for 2 hours. Remove
from freezer, blend until smooth and re-
freeze. Remove from freezer 5 minutes
before serving and garnish with fresh
mint.

Serves 4

PISA PEACHES

1 cup pine nuts
1 cup currants
1 teaspoon cinnamon
4 fresh golden peaches, halved and
 stoned
2 cups sweet Marsala

Preheat oven to 180°C (375°F). Blend
together pine nuts, currants and
cinnamon. Stuff blended mixture into
cavity of peach halves. Place peaches
cut side up in non-stick baking dish and
pour over Marsala. Bake for 25 minutes
and serve.

Serves 4

STRAWBERRY GELATO

4 cups fresh strawberries, hulled
1 cup water
1 cup lemon juice
1 tablespoon gelatine mixed with
 2 tablespoons hot water

Puree strawberries. Add all other
ingredients and blend or beat until well
combined. Pour into ice-cream trays and
freeze for 2 hours. Remove from freezer,
blend until smooth and re-freeze.
Remove from freezer 5 minutes before
serving.

Serves 4–6

Sasaki Black Grid Lock plate

Strawberry Gelato and Peach Gelato

ROCK MELON GELATO

1 medium-sized rock melon, peeled
 and seeded
1 cup water
½ cup lemon juice
1 tablespoon gelatine mixed with
 2 tablespoons hot water

Puree rock melon. Add all other
ingredients and blend or beat until well
combined. Pour into ice-cream trays and
freeze for 2 hours. Remove from freezer,
blend until smooth and re-freeze.
Remove from freezer 5 minutes before
serving.

Serves 4–6

RICOTTA CAKE

BASE
1 cup raw oats, blended into coarse
 crumbs
1 teaspoon freshly grated nutmeg
3 tablespoons apple juice
 concentrate

CAKE FILLING
1 cup currants, marinated in ½ cup
 sweet Marsala for 30 minutes
500 g (1 lb) fresh ricotta cheese, well
 drained
2 egg whites
1 tablespoon finely grated lemon zest
1 tablespoon finely grated orange
 zest
1 tablespoon gelatine mixed with 2
 tablespoons hot water
½ teaspoon vanilla essence

Preheat oven to 180°C (375°F). Combine
base ingredients and press into the
bottom of a non-stick dish. Refrigerate for
1 hour.
 Remove currants from Marsala and
drain. Add currants to other filling
ingredients. Beat or blend until smooth
and creamy. Pour into 20 cm (8 in) dish
and bake for 40 minutes. Cool,
refrigerate, slice and serve.

Serves 4–6

THE BEST OF BRITISH

Pork pies, steak and kidney pudding, treacle tart, peas and chips — if you think that's all there is to British food your taste buds are in for a culinary revolution.

When I visited London recently it seemed as if the gourmet delights of the world were crammed into their magnificent food halls. Delicacies from many countries now influence the way meals are prepared and cooked.

Try our Pritikin-style adaptations of traditional favourites like Shepherds' Pie and Cock a Leekie, or sophisticated recipes like Highland Fruit Salad with strawberries in brandy and cinnamon. *Cheers!*

SHEPHERDS' PIE

2 kg (4¼ lb) potatoes, peeled and chopped
1 cup defatted beef or vegetable stock (see recipe)
1 bay leaf
2 onions, finely sliced
3 cloves garlic, finely sliced
1 kg (2 lb 2 oz) lean minced topside beef
1 egg white, lightly beaten
1 tablespoon tomato paste mixed with 1 tablespoon water
1 tablespoon chopped fresh parsley
freshly ground black pepper
2 tablespoons white wine
½ cup skim milk
1 teaspoon grated Geska cheese

Preheat oven to 190°C (375°F). Steam or boil chopped potatoes until tender, then mash and set aside.

In a pan, bring stock to the boil. Add bay leaf, onions and garlic. Reduce heat, cover and simmer for 5 minutes. Add meat, egg white, tomato paste and water, parsley, pepper and wine, mix well and simmer for a further 10 minutes. Drain off excess liquid and set aside. Remove bay leaf.

Combine potatoes with skim milk and Geska cheese. Place meat mixture in large ovenproof dish. Spoon over mashed potato and bake for 1 hour.

Serves 4–6

SCOTCH BROTH

1 cup water
1 large onion, sliced
1 leek, white part only, thinly sliced
8 cups defatted beef or vegetable stock (see recipe)
1 cup fresh peas
3 carrots, peeled and grated
1 turnip, peeled and diced
¼ cup diced celery
½ small cabbage, finely shredded
1 cup pearl barley
freshly ground black pepper
500 g (1 lb) beef or lamb fillet, trimmed of all visible fat and thinly sliced
¼ cup finely chopped fresh parsley

Bring water to the boil, add onion and leek. Reduce heat, cover and simmer for 5 minutes. Add all other ingredients except beef and parsley. Bring to the boil, reduce heat, cover and simmer for 15 minutes.

Add beef slices and simmer for another 30 minutes on a low heat. Stir in chopped parsley. Heat through and serve with wholemeal Pritikin bread.

Serves 4–6

LEEKS WITH CHEESE SAUCE

1 cup water
4 medium-sized leeks, washed, trimmed and sliced in half lengthways
¼ cup finely chopped fresh parsley, for garnish

CHEESE SAUCE
1 cup ricotta cheese
¾ cup skim milk
1 tablespoon grated Geska cheese
freshly ground black pepper

Bring water to the boil and add leeks. Reduce heat, cover and simmer for 8 minutes. Remove from pan, drain and chill.

To make the sauce, blend all the ingredients and chill. Just before serving, pour over leeks and garnish with parsley.

Serves 4

Shepherds' Pie

PEASE PUDDING

500 g (1 lb) split peas, yellow or green
1 onion, finely sliced
1 bay leaf
freshly ground black pepper
1 egg white
2 teaspoons finely chopped fresh
parsley

Rinse split peas well. Cover with water and soak overnight. Rinse and drain. Cover soaked peas with 2½ cups water. Add onion, bay leaf and pepper. Bring to the boil, cover and simmer for 1¼ hours. Remove lid and simmer for a further 15 minutes.

Stir through egg white and parsley and heat through. Puree and serve.

Serves 4–6

COCK A LEEKIE

1.5 kg (3 lb) boiling chicken, skinned
12 cups water
1 bay leaf
freshly ground black pepper
1 large white onion, finely chopped
1 kg (2 lb 2 oz) leeks, trimmed and
finely chopped
1 tablespoon finely chopped fresh
parsley
500 g (1 lb) pitted prunes

Place chicken and water in a large saucepan with the bay leaf, pepper, onion and half the leeks. Bring to the boil, cover and simmer for 1½ hours. Strain off soup. Allow chicken to cool, and remove about 2 cups of flesh. Roughly chop.

Return stock to pan with remaining leeks, and cook for another 10 minutes. Stir in chicken flesh and chopped parsley.

Place several prunes in each bowl and pour in soup. Serve with wholemeal Pritikin bread.

Serves 4–6

OATMEAL FISH FRY

4 egg whites, lightly beaten
2 teaspoons finely chopped fresh
parsley
freshly ground black pepper
1 kg (2 lb 2 oz) fish fillets, rinsed and
patted dry
3 cups raw oats blended until flour is
medium to fine
lemon wedges, for garnish

Preheat non-stick frypan. Combine egg whites with parsley and pepper. Roll fish fillets in egg white, then press firmly into oatmeal. Roll again in egg white, then place in non-stick frypan. Cook on both sides until brown. Serve with lemon wedges and salad.

Serves 4–6

TATTY POT

1 cup water
2 white onions, finely sliced
1 cup cottage cheese
1 teaspoon grated Geska cheese
1½ cups skim milk
1 kg (2 lb 2 oz) potatoes, peeled and
thinly sliced
1 teaspoon dried sage
freshly ground black pepper

Preheat oven to 190°C (375°F). Bring water to the boil and add onions. Reduce heat, cover and simmer for 5 minutes. Drain and set aside. Puree cottage and Geska cheese with skim milk. Combine well with onions.

Layer potatoes in large ovenproof dish. Pour over cheese, milk and onion mixture. Sprinkle with dried sage and pepper. Bake for 1 hour.

Serves 4–6

HIGHLAND FRUIT SALAD

1 kg (2 lb 2 oz) combined fresh
strawberries, blackcurrants and
raspberries
juice 1 orange
2 tablespoons brandy
dash ground cinnamon

Combine all ingredients. Serve with low-fat yoghurt.

Serves 4–6

Selection of fruits for Highland Fruit Salad

CURRANT SCONES

4 cups raw oats, blended to a fine
flour
3 teaspoons baking powder
½ teaspoon mixed spice
¾ cup currants, rinsed under cold
water and drained well
1 cup skim milk

Preheat oven to 220°C (425°F). Combine oat flour with baking powder, mixed spice and currants. Pour in milk and knead lightly to form dough. Roll out to thickness of 2.5 cm (1 in). Use a scone cutter or glass jar, lightly floured, to cut out scone rounds.

Place on non-stick baking tray and brush tops with extra skim milk. Bake for 12 minutes. Wrap cooked scones in clean tea towel until required. Serve with thick fruit puree and low-fat yoghurt or Ricotta Whip (see recipe). If not eaten immediately, reheat in oven for 1 minute before serving.

Makes 10–12

FRUIT LOAF

250 g (8 oz) sultanas
125 g (4 oz) raisins, chopped
125 g (4 oz) dried apricots, chopped
¼ cup water
1 cup raw oats
1 cup skim milk
2 egg whites, stiffly beaten
1 teaspoon ground ginger
1½ cups wholemeal self-raising flour

Place fruit in saucepan with water. Simmer on low heat for 3 minutes and allow to cool. Blend oats until finely ground, place in a bowl with skim milk and allow to stand for 1 hour.

Preheat oven to 180°C (350°F). Fold egg whites and ginger into oat and milk mixture. Add fruit and flour alternately and stir until well combined. Pour into a 28 cm × 10 cm (11 in × 4 in) non-stick loaf tin and bake for 50 minutes. Allow to stand in tin for 10 minutes, then lift out and place on cake rack to cool.

GIFTS FROM GREECE

Greece is fascinating, whether you're digging for ancient ruins or edible treats. Each region offers specialities which are hard to resist.

Local food relies on the freshest possible produce and fresh herbs are always preferred. Many dishes are flavoured with dill, parsley, garlic, thyme, mint and sage. Yoghurt, rice and salad are often served as side dishes.

More substantial recipes like Moussaka and Souvlakia will already be familiar to many culinary enthusiasts. Less well known and equally delicious are dishes such as Egg and Lemon Soup, Vegetable Stew and Grape Juice Pudding.

Kali orexi!

CHEESE PIE

150 g (5 oz) cottage cheese
1 tablespoon grated Geska cheese
1 egg white, lightly beaten
2 tablespoons chopped fresh parsley
dash nutmeg
freshly ground black pepper
¼ cup skim milk
12 sheets filo pastry

Combine cottage and Geska cheeses with egg white, parsley, nutmeg and pepper. Preheat oven to 190°C (375°F).

Layer a round 20 cm (8 in) non-stick baking tin with 6 folded sheets of filo. Brush each sheet separately with skim milk. Pour in cheese mixture and press flat. Top with remaining folded layers of pastry. Brush each sheet with milk.

Trim overlapping pastry edges with scissors and tuck in firmly. Brush top of pie with extra milk. Bake for 30 minutes. Cut into wedges and serve.

Serves 4–6

YOGHURT DIP

1 medium-sized cucumber
3 cloves garlic, minced
2 cups low-fat yoghurt
2 teaspoons vinegar
2 teaspoons chopped fresh mint
freshly ground black pepper

Peel and dice cucumber and stand in strainer to drain excess liquid. Combine all ingredients, chill and serve.

Serves 4–6

SOUVLAKIA

1 kg (2 lb 2 oz) beef or lamb fillets, trimmed of all visible fat and diced

MARINADE
2 tablespoons fresh oregano or 2 teaspoons dried oregano
3 garlic cloves, finely chopped
juice 2 lemons
1 cup dry white wine
freshly ground black pepper

Combine marinade ingredients and marinate beef overnight. Thread onto metal or bamboo skewers. (Pre-soak bamboo skewers overnight in water to prevent burning.) Grill for 15–20 minutes basting regularly with marinade. Serve with salad.

Serves 4–6

FISH PIQUANT

1 kg (2 lb 2 oz) fish fillets or whole fish
1 heaped tablespoon wholemeal flour
1 cup water
2 garlic cloves, minced
¼ cup wine vinegar
2 teaspoons chopped fresh rosemary
freshly ground black pepper

Grill fish until it flakes. Set aside and keep warm.

Mix flour with water. Add garlic, vinegar, rosemary and pepper. Bring to the boil, stirring continuously. Reduce heat, simmer and stir sauce for 2–3 minutes. Pour over grilled fish and serve with salad and brown rice.

Serves 4–6

Souvlakia

BAKED FISH WITH GARLIC

1 whole fish, at least 800 g (1 lb 8 oz)
8 cloves garlic, minced
juice 1 lemon
1 tablespoon vinegar
¼ cup chopped fresh parsley
1 teaspoon dried marjoram
freshly ground black pepper

Preheat oven to 190°C (375°F). Rinse fish, pat dry and place on a sheet of foil.

Combine garlic with lemon juice, vinegar, parsley, marjoram and pepper and pour over fish. Wrap up fish in foil, place in baking dish and bake for 40 minutes. Serve with salad.

Serves 4–6

MOUSSAKA

3 large eggplants, about 1.5 kg (3 lb)
MEAT SAUCE
½ cup water
2 large white onions, finely chopped
3 garlic cloves, chopped
1 kg (2 lb 2 oz) lean minced topside beef
3 tablespoons tomato paste mixed with ¼ cup water
2 very ripe tomatoes, chopped
¼ cup chopped fresh parsley
½ cup red or white wine
1 teaspoon cinnamon
freshly ground black pepper

WHITE SAUCE
6 tablespoons wholemeal flour
4 cups skim milk
4 egg whites
1 tablespoon grated Geska cheese
dash nutmeg

Preheat oven to 180°C (350°F). Cut eggplants into medium-sized slices. Place on kitchen paper for 20 minutes to absorb bitter juices, then rinse and pat dry. Steam until tender and set aside.

To make meat sauce, bring water to the boil and add onions and garlic. Reduce heat, cover and simmer for 5 minutes. Add meat and saute for a further 5 minutes. Add remaining meat sauce ingredients. Cover and simmer for 20 minutes on low heat. Drain off excess liquid and set aside.

To make white sauce, mix flour and milk. Bring to the boil, stirring continuously for 2 minutes. Add egg whites, Geska and nutmeg. Cook for a further 2 minutes.

Layer a 24 cm × 31 cm × 5 cm (10 in × 12 in × 2 in) ovenproof dish alternately with eggplant and meat mixture, topping with eggplant. Pour over white sauce and bake for 1 hour. Allow to stand for several minutes before cutting.

Serves 4–6

VEGETABLE STEW

¼ cup water
1 onion, sliced
3 garlic cloves, chopped
3 medium-sized zucchini, sliced
3 medium-sized potatoes, peeled and sliced
125 g fresh peas
3 very ripe tomatoes, chopped
1 teaspoon tomato paste
1 carrot, peeled and sliced
1 bay leaf
freshly ground black pepper
1 green capsicum, seeded and sliced
1 teaspoon chopped fresh dill
1 tablespoon chopped fresh parsley

Bring water to the boil and add onion and garlic. Reduce heat, cover and simmer for 5 minutes. Add all other ingredients except capsicum, dill and parsley. Cover and simmer on low heat for 15 minutes. Add capsicum, dill and parsley and simmer for a further 10 minutes. Serve hot.

Serves 4–6

GREEK SALAD

1 cos lettuce, broken into pieces
2 tomatoes, sliced in wedges
1 small cucumber, sliced
4 radishes, sliced
1 small green capsicum, seeded and sliced
1 small white onion, sliced
125 g (4 oz) ricotta cheese, cut in chunks

DRESSING
1 cup fresh orange juice
1 teaspoon lemon juice
1 teaspoon vinegar
1 clove garlic, minced
1 teaspoon dried oregano
freshly ground black pepper

Arrange salad ingredients in bowl. Combine dressing ingredients, pour over salad and serve.

Serves 4–6

CHICKEN PIE

1.5 kg (3 lb) chicken breasts, skinned and roughly chopped
2 large white onions, chopped
2 bay leaves
2 garlic cloves, chopped
2 tablespoons chopped fresh parsley
freshly ground black pepper
2½ cups water
12 sheets filo pastry
¼ cup skim milk

SAUCE
4 tablespoons wholemeal flour
1½ cups skim milk
1 tablespoon grated Geska cheese
4 lightly beaten egg whites
dash nutmeg

Preheat oven to 190°C (375°F). Place chicken, onions, bay leaves, garlic, parsley, pepper and water in pan. Bring to boil. Reduce heat, cover and simmer for 20 minutes. Drain, remove bay leaves and set aside.

To make sauce, combine flour and milk and bring to the boil, stirring continuously. Reduce heat. Stir in cheese, egg whites and nutmeg. Pour over chicken mixture and allow to cool. Blend for a few seconds only.

Line an ovenproof dish with six layers of filo pastry. Brush each sheet separately with skim milk. Pour in chicken mixture and top with remaining pastry sheets. Sprinkle with extra skim milk.

Trim off overlapping filo pastry with scissors. Tuck in pastry around edges. Bake for 30 minutes.

Serves 4–6

BEETROOT SALAD

500 g (1 lb) fresh beetroot
chopped parsley, for garnish

DRESSING
1 tablespoon vinegar
¼ cup fresh orange juice
2 cloves garlic, minced
squeeze lemon juice
freshly ground black pepper

Remove beetroot tops. Steam beetroot for 20 minutes, peel and dice. Combine dressing ingredients and add to diced beetroot. Chill, garnish with parsley and serve.

Serves 4–6

Greek Salad

LENTIL SOUP

2½ cups yellow lentils
1 celery stalk, including 2–3 leaves,
chopped
1 large onion, chopped
3 bay leaves
2 garlic cloves, chopped
7 cups water
freshly ground black pepper
1 tablespoon vinegar

Rinse lentils. Combine with all other ingredients except vinegar and bring to the boil. Reduce heat, cover and simmer for 45 minutes. Remove bay leaves, add vinegar and puree soup in blender. Reheat and serve.

Serves 4–6

EGG AND LEMON SOUP

6 cups defatted chicken or fish stock
(see recipe)
½ cup brown rice
3 egg whites, lightly beaten
juice 1 lemon
freshly ground black pepper
1 lemon, thinly sliced, for garnish

Bring stock to the boil and add rice. Cover, reduce heat and simmer for 40 minutes.

Combine egg whites with lemon juice and 1 cup hot soup. Stir into soup. Heat through, add pepper, garnish with lemon slices and serve.

Serves 4–6

ZUCCHINI SALAD

1 kg (2 lb 2 oz) zucchini thinly sliced
juice 1 lemon
juice 2 oranges
1 clove garlic, chopped
1 small white onion, chopped
1 tablespoon chopped fresh parsley
freshly ground black pepper

Combine all ingredients. Chill and serve.

Serves 4–6

Lentil Soup

TOMATOES STUFFED

8 medium-sized tomatoes
2 tablespoons lightly toasted pine nuts
1 large white onion, finely chopped
freshly ground black pepper
1 cup cooked brown rice
2 tablespoons finely chopped fresh parsley
1 tablespoon finely chopped fresh mint
1 tablespoon currants
1 cup water
juice 1 lemon

Preheat oven to 180°C (350°F). Slice tops off tomatoes and set aside. Scoop out pulp and mix with pine nuts, onion and pepper. Add to non-stick pan and simmer for 5 minutes. Stir in rice, parsley, mint and currants and heat through.

Pile mixture into tomato cases and replace sliced off tops. Put tomatoes in ovenproof dish. Pour in 1 cup water and lemon juice. Bake for 30 minutes and serve.

Serves 4–6

PRAWNS WITH RICOTTA CHEESE

125 g (4 oz) fresh ricotta cheese
½ cup water
2 large white onions, chopped
3 garlic cloves, chopped
3 cups chopped very ripe tomatoes
1 tablespoon tomato paste
1 cup white wine
2 tablespoons chopped fresh parsley
1 teaspoon dried oregano
freshly ground black pepper
1 kg (2 lb 2 oz) large uncooked prawns, shelled and deveined, leaving tails on

Dice ricotta cheese and lightly toast under griller. Set aside. Bring water to the boil. Add onions and garlic. Reduce heat and simmer for 3–4 minutes. Add tomatoes, tomato paste, white wine, parsley, oregano and pepper. Cover and simmer for 30 minutes. Add prawns and cook for 12 minutes until tender. Top with ricotta cheese cubes and garnish with extra chopped parsley.

Serves 4–6

GRAPE JUICE PUDDING

This is a healthy adaptation of a popular Greek dessert.

2 cups raw oats
3 cups unsweetened grape juice
1 tablespoon apple juice concentrate
½ teaspoon mixed spice
low-fat yoghurt and grated orange zest, for garnish

Mix oats with 1 cup grape juice and the apple juice concentrate. Bring remaining 2 cups grape juice to the boil. Reduce heat, add oat mixture and mixed spice. Simmer and stir continuously for 5 minutes. Pour into individual small bowls and chill for 1–2 hours in refrigerator. Unmould and serve with low-fat yoghurt and grated orange zest.

Serves 4–6

RICE PUDDING

3 cups brown rice
4 cups skim milk mixed with 2 teaspoons wholemeal flour
1 teaspoon vanilla essence
1 teaspoon ground cinnamon
1 teaspoon grated lemon zest
¼ cup apple juice concentrate
1 cup raisins, rinsed under cold water and drained

Rinse rice. Cover with cold water and bring to the boil. Reduce heat, cover and simmer gently for 10 minutes. Combine parboiled rice with all other ingredients except raisins. Bring to the boil, cover and simmer on a very low heat for 40 minutes. Stir in raisins and serve.

Serves 4–6

Grape Juice Pudding

MIDDLE EASTERN CUISINE

Middle Eastern cuisine is wonderful and surprisingly simple to prepare. Specialties include freshly baked pita bread, lean lamb kebabs, hoummos, salads and garden fruits. Pile on the fresh herbs — parsley, dill, mint and garlic. Traditional dishes often include lamb, but you can substitute lean beef, chicken, fish or vegetables. Many of the following recipes keep well for at least two days.

IRANIAN STUFFED CHICKEN

¼ cup water
1 small white onion, chopped
400 g (13 oz) lean minced beef
1½ cups cooked brown rice
½ teaspoon mixed spice
1 tablespoon lightly toasted pine nuts (optional)
2 bay leaves
100 g (3½ oz) mixed dried fruit, rinsed under cold water and drained
2 teaspoons finely chopped fresh parsley
freshly ground black pepper
1.6 kg (3 lb 3 oz) chicken, skinned
¼ cup lemon juice

Preheat oven to 200°C (400°F). Bring water to the boil in non-stick frypan. Add onion, cover and simmer for 5 minutes. Remove from pan. Add beef and saute for 5 minutes. Combine beef and onion with rice, mixed spice, pine nuts, bay leaves, dried fruit, parsley and pepper and mix thoroughly.

Stuff mixture into cavity of chicken. Truss with skewer and brush with lemon juice. Cover with foil and bake for 40 minutes. Reduce heat to 180°C (350°F). Remove foil and cook for a further 40 minutes until brown. Serve with vegetables or salad.

Serves 4–6

HOUMMOS

125 g (4 oz) dried chick peas
5 cloves garlic, chopped
½ cup toasted sesame seeds (optional)
juice 3 lemons
1 teaspoon paprika
fresh parsley sprigs, for garnish

Soak chick peas overnight and discard skins. Boil the soaked chick peas for 1 hour and drain. Blend with garlic until smooth and set aside. Blend sesame seeds until smooth and add to chick peas and garlic. Stir in lemon juice. Sprinkle with paprika. Garnish with parsley and serve with wholemeal pita bread.

Note: The name of this well-known recipe can be spelt in several ways e.g. hummus and hommos.

Serves 4–6

TABOULI SALAD

1 cup finely ground burghul (cracked wheat)
1 large bunch fresh parsley, finely chopped (remove stalks)
½ cup finely chopped fresh mint
1 small white onion, finely diced
juice 3–4 lemons
freshly ground black pepper
3 tomatoes, seeded and diced
lettuce leaves, for garnish

Cover burghul with cold water and soak for 30 minutes. Drain and press out excess water. Mix burghul with all other ingredients except tomatoes. Top with diced tomatoes and serve with lettuce leaves.

Note: The name of this famous dish can be spelt in a variety of ways e.g. tabouleh and tabbouli.

Serves 4–6

Iranian Stuffed Chicken

EGGPLANT AND YOGHURT SALAD

1 large eggplant
1 cup water or stock
3 cloves garlic, finely chopped
2 teaspoons finely chopped fresh mint
1½ cups low-fat yoghurt
freshly ground black pepper

Dice eggplant and place on kitchen paper for 20 minutes to absorb bitter juices. Rinse and pat dry. Bring stock to the boil and add eggplant. Cover and simmer until tender. Remove from pan, drain and cool. Mix garlic and mint with yoghurt. Stir in eggplant and pepper. Chill and serve.

Serves 4–6

FISH AND CRACKED WHEAT PATTIES

1 cup finely ground burghul (cracked wheat)
500 g (1 lb) fish fillets, skinned
1 medium-sized white onion, chopped
3 cloves garlic, chopped
1 cup chopped fresh coriander or parsley
½ teaspoon cayenne pepper
freshly ground black pepper
1 lightly beaten egg white
lemon wedges, for garnish

Soak burghul in cold water for 30 minutes. Drain well and press out all water. Blend fish, onion and garlic until smooth. Mix in bowl with chopped coriander, peppers and egg white.

Take small amounts of mixture and form into flattish patties. Preheat non-stick frypan and cook patties until brown (about 8 minutes each side). Garnish with lemon wedges and serve.

Serves 4–6

Fish and Cracked Wheat Patties

TURKISH WEDDING SOUP

500 g (1 lb) lean beef or lamb, trimmed of excess fat and diced
¼ cup wholemeal flour
¼ cup water
1 bay leaf
1 carrot, peeled and chopped
1 onion, chopped
freshly ground black pepper
8 cups vegetable stock (see recipe)
3 egg whites
juice 1 lemon
2 teaspoons finely chopped fresh parsley
4 teaspoons paprika

Roll diced meat in flour. Bring water to the boil, add meat and saute for 5 minutes. Add bay leaf, carrot, onion, pepper and vegetable stock. Simmer covered on low heat for 1½ hours. Skim surface. Remove meat and set aside. Strain soup and keep warm.

Mix egg whites with lemon juice and 1 cup hot soup. Pour into soup pot and add meat. Reheat, but don't bring to the boil. Sprinkle with parsley and paprika and serve.

Serves 4–6

BABA GHANOUSH

2 medium-sized eggplants
4 cloves garlic
¾ cup fresh lemon juice
1 teaspoon ground cumin
freshly ground black pepper
2 tablespoons lightly toasted sesame seeds (optional)
chopped fresh parsley and tomato wedges, for garnish

Preheat griller or set oven at 180°C (350°F). Grill or bake eggplants until skin blisters and turns black. Peel eggplants while hot. Roughly chop flesh, puree it and set aside.

Finely chop or blend garlic and stir into eggplant puree. Add lemon juice, cumin and pepper. Blend sesame seeds to a paste and swirl through puree. Garnish with parsley and tomato wedges and serve with wholemeal crackers or pita bread.

Serves 4–6

LEBANESE LADIES FINGERS

1 large bunch spinach
1 cup vegetable or defatted chicken stock (see recipe)
1 medium-sized white onion, finely chopped
½ teaspoon freshly grated nutmeg
½ teaspoon cinnamon
1 teaspoon finely chopped fresh dill
freshly ground black pepper
6 sheets filo pastry, cut in half
½ cup skim milk
fresh parsley sprigs and lemon wedges, for garnish

Remove white stalks of spinach, including centre stalk. Finely chop remaining leaves.

Preheat oven to 190°C (375°F). Bring stock to the boil and add onion. Reduce heat, cover and simmer for 5 minutes. Add chopped spinach, cover and simmer for 4 minutes. Remove spinach from pan. Drain off all excess liquid. Add nutmeg, cinnamon, dill and pepper to spinach and mix until well combined. Allow to cool.

Take small amount of mixture and place along lower edge of one sheet of pastry. Roll up about half-way. Fold in edges like an envelope and neatly roll up completely. Seal edges with dash of skim milk. Repeat process twelve times. Sprinkle rolls with skim milk. Place on non-stick baking tray and bake for 35 minutes until brown. Garnish with parsley and lemon wedges and serve.

Serves 4–6

FALAFEL

500 g (1 lb) dried chick peas
4 cloves garlic
6 shallots
1 bunch fresh parsley, stalks removed
1 teaspoon cayenne pepper
freshly ground black pepper
1½ teaspoons freshly ground coriander
2 teaspoons freshly ground cumin
4 egg whites, lightly beaten
lemon wedges, for garnish

Soak chick peas overnight, rinse and discard skins. Grind chick peas until they resemble fine crumbs.

Preheat oven to 200°C (400°F). Blend garlic, shallots and parsley until smooth. Add ground chick peas to garlic mixture. Combine with peppers, coriander, cumin and 2 egg whites.

Take small amounts of mixture, knead well and roll into small balls. Brush with remaining beaten egg whites and place on non-stick baking tray. Bake for 30 minutes until brown. Serve with tabouli salad, low-fat yoghurt, lemon wedges and wholemeal pita bread.

Serves 4–6

STUFFED EGGPLANT

2 medium-sized eggplants
2 cloves garlic, halved
¼ cup water
1 onion, finely chopped
400 g (13 oz) lean minced beef
2 tablespoons chopped fresh parsley
1 cup cooked brown rice or cooked fresh peas
1 tablespoon tomato paste
1 teaspoon mixed spice
1 tablespoon lemon juice
1 tablespoon toasted pine nuts (optional)
freshly ground black pepper
1 egg white, lightly beaten
6 very ripe tomatoes, pureed

Preheat oven to 190°C (375°F). Cut eggplants in half lengthwise, scoop out pulp and save for salads. Rub garlic halves around inside of eggplant shells to help remove bitter juices. Leave for 20 minutes then rinse and dry eggplant shells.

Bring water to the boil and add onion. Reduce heat, cover and simmer for 5 minutes. Add meat and saute for a further 8 minutes. Add parsley, rice, tomato paste, mixed spice and lemon juice and cook for a further 2–3 minutes. Drain off excess pan juices and set aside.

Place mixture in eggplant shells with pine nuts, pepper and egg white and put into ovenproof dish. Pour over tomato puree. Pour pan juices into bottom of dish and add a little extra water. Bake for 30 minutes.

Serves 4–6

EATING WELL PRITIKIN-STYLE

"I'd rather die than eat this rabbit food." That was my father's initial response to the Pritikin eating plan, even though he had suffered three heart attacks, and was frequently reduced to tears by angina pain. Furthermore, he was facing — with great reluctance — the prospect of open heart surgery.

My 'classic Pritikin' response to his remark was: "Well, Dad if you would rather die than change your diet, you will!"

Five years later and after much cajoling from me, my father now swims two kilometres a day, takes no medication, and his doctors refer to his reversal of heart disease as nothing short of 'miraculous'.

The 'miracle maker' in this instance was Nathan Pritikin. He was diagnosed as having heart disease when in his early forties. Depressed by the prospect of long-term medication, he began investigating possible links between diet and heart disease. After studying the eating habits of many nations, he found that people who ate a diet low in animal protein and high in complex carbohydrates — whole grains, fruit and vegetables — were relatively free from heart disease, cancer, diabetes and arthritis.

Pritikin threw away his pills, started eating 'real, naturally grown food' and drastically reduced his intake of fatty foods. He cured himself of heart disease and set out to prove to the rest of the Western world that we are eating ourselves to death.

He then founded the Pritikin Longevity Centre in Santa Monica, California and became a legendary figure in the health area.

In 1980 I was the Public Relations Manager for Schwartz Publishing which first introduced the Pritikin concept to Australia by publishing *The Pritikin Program for Diet and Exercise* in hardcover. My job was to promote the book and its author.

When I first presented Nathan with a publicity campaign itinerary comprising more than 120 interviews, I apologised that we would really be 'on the run'. He left me gasping as he raced up television studio staircases, bolted into fruit shops during breaks to buy bananas — well ripened ones — and every interview was as fresh as the first. The many journalists who interviewed Nathan repeatedly whispered to me: "He's incredibly energetic and looks 20 years younger than his real age."

During those exciting three weeks with Nathan Pritikin I was given a verbal crash course in nutrition. It changed my life.

What I will never forget about Nathan Pritikin was his humble approach, unstinting dedication to curing and preventing disease, and his personal kindness and good humour.

THE PRITIKIN LIFETIME EATING PLAN

The Pritikin eating plan embraces a maintenance diet and a regression diet.

Maintenance Diet: for people without a medical condition. This diet is now described by the Pritikin Longevity Centre as the Pritikin Lifetime Eating Plan. On this plan, eighty per cent of your kilojoules should come from complex carbohydrates — whole grains, vegetables and fruit. Ten per cent of kilojoules should come from fats found in foods such as chicken and lean meats; and ten per cent should come from protein — lean meats, fish, chicken, skim milk dairy products, peas and beans. Eat only 84–112 grams (3-4 oz) of animal protein per day, with a maximum of 680 grams (22 oz) per week.

Under recent modifications to this diet, twenty-five per cent of your daily carbohydrate intake may come from refined grain products; fruit is now unlimited for those without overweight or triglyceride problems; and fish is recommended as the first choice of animal proteins, as it is lower in saturated fatty acids and helps to reduce a tendency to blood clotting, which can cause heart attack or stroke. Ultra low-fat cheeses, such as some mozzarella or cheddar which have no more than 34 per cent of their calories from fat, may also be used as a meat substitute but in smaller quantities — 60 grams (2 oz) cheese to replace the 100 gram (3½ oz) portion of fish, poultry or lean meat.

Regression Diet: recommended for people suffering from heart disease, obesity, severe arthritis and other degenerative diseases. This diet is now called a 'therapeutic modification' of the Pritikin Lifetime Eating Plan. Under this eating plan, limit yourself to a maximum of 100 grams (3½ oz) of animal protein per week and follow the guidelines of the Pritikin Lifetime Eating Plan.

You don't need to keep charts or count kilojoules. Once you start eating a diet consisting largely of whole grains, vegetables and fruit with only small portions of protein, you will develop an instinct about the correct diet to ensure good health. Your taste buds will rediscover the delectable flavours of food unadulterated by salt, sugar and fat, and you may never again be tempted by 'dangerous foods' that can kill you.

The recipes contained in this book are low in fat, cholesterol and protein, with no added salt, sugar or oil.

The recipes conform to the healthy eating principles outlined in the following bestselling books.
The Pritikin Program for Diet and Exercise by Nathan Pritikin with Patrick M. McGrady (Bantam, 1981).
The Pritikin Promise — 28 Days to a Longer, Healthier Life by Nathan Pritikin (Bantam, 1985).

The Pritikin organisation in the U.S.A. is constantly updating its guidelines as new information about nutrition becomes available. The latest method of simplifying the Pritikin recommendations, is to divide food into three categories: 'Go' (foods to eat); 'Caution' (foods to eat in small quantities or only occasionally); and 'Stop' (foods to avoid). These are set out in an easy reference chart below, reproduced courtesy of *The Pritikin Lifestyle*, the monthly newsletter of The Pritikin Health Association of Australia.

THE THREE FOOD CATEGORIES

Go

The green light signals the healthiest food
choices. All foods listed in this group are
recommended on the Pritikin Lifetime
Eating Plan.

FOOD	INCLUDES	RECOMMENDED AMOUNTS
Beverages	Any type of mineral water, hot grain drinks, vegetable and fruit juices, and selected herbal teas.	Unlimited quantities of everything on list except fruit juice (*see Fruit*).
Dairy	Nonfat plain yoghurt, nonfat or skim milk, nonfat cheese such as cottage or ricotta cheese (both no more than 1% fat by weight).	Two servings of nonfat dairy products daily. A serving is about 377 kilojoules (90 calories) or 1 cup skim milk, ¾ cup nonfat yoghurt or 60 grams (2 oz) ricotta or cottage cheese (1% or lower fat by weight).
Fish, shellfish, lean fowl, lean red meat, egg whites	Fish is preferred over fowl, and fowl is recommended over red meat. Use skinned white meat of poultry.	Up to 100 grams (3½ oz) protein daily. A serving has about 418–836 kilojoules (100–200 calories). Clams, oysters and scallops may be eaten in this amount but portions of lobster, crab and prawns should be reduced to 60 grams (2 oz). If desired, 1½ cups cooked beans, 185 grams (6 oz) tofu or 60 grams (2 oz) ultra low-fat cheese (less than 34% kilojoules from fat) may be substituted for animal protein. You can eat up to 7 egg whites a week.
Fruit	Whole fruit, fresh or frozen, is preferred; fruit canned in its own juice, dried fruit, fruit juice, and fruit juice concentrate are acceptable.	Three or more servings of whole fruit daily. A serving = 1 fruit or about 250 kilojoules (60 calories). Fruit juice (½ cup) or fruit juice concentrate (2 tablespoons) may be substituted for up to one-third of fruit servings.
Legumes	Peas and beans, for example, chick peas, green peas, lentils, and black, brown, pink and pinto beans.	A sensible amount; *see Whole grains*.
Nuts	Chestnuts (small quantities pine nuts are optional).	A sensible amount; *see Whole grains*.
Soybean products	Cooked soybeans and tofu (up to 55% of calories from fat).	Useful substitutes for meat; maximum of 185 grams (6 oz) daily.

Vegetables	Fresh or frozen vegetables as desired, without added salt or fat. For example: broccoli, carrots, lettuce, onions and tomatoes.	Four or more servings of raw vegetable salad and/or cooked vegetables daily. A serving is approximately 105 kilojoules (25 calories), about 1 cup raw vegetables or ½ cup of cooked vegetables. Include dark green and yellow or orange vegetables daily. Vegetable juice may be substituted for up to one-quarter of vegetable servings.
Whole grains	All whole grains and whole grain products such as breads, cereals and crackers prepared with acceptable Pritikin ingredients. For example, whole grain bread, whole wheat spaghetti, oatmeal, rice crackers. Refined grains and grain products, such as white flour, white rice, and white bread, may be eaten provided they do not exceed one-quarter of total calories.	Four or more servings of whole grains daily (wheat, oats, rye, corn, brown rice, barley, buckwheat) in the form of cereal, side dishes, pasta or bread. A serving is approximately 335 kilojoules (80 calories). Chestnuts, beans and peas, and starchy vegetables, such as potatoes, yams, and winter squashes may be substituted for some of the grain servings.

Caution

Yellow signals caution. The less consumed the better. If these foods are consumed occasionally and/or in small amounts, they pose little danger. People with cardiovascular disease or other medical problems should be especially cautious in using any of these foods. The food groups are listed here in order of increasing risk to your health, with the least harmful group listed first.

FOOD	INCLUDES
Sweeteners	Molasses, barley malt, honey, maple syrup, rice syrup, corn syrup, all refined sugars.
Water-processed decaffinated coffee and tea	
Aspartame	An artificial sweetener.
Fruits	Olives and avocados.
Unsalted nuts	Walnuts, almonds, pumpkin kernels, pecans, pistachios, sunflower seeds, filberts, sesame seeds, brazil nuts, peanuts.
Low sodium soy sauce and miso	
Alcoholic beverages	Dry white wines preferred.
Dairy	Low-fat yoghurt, low-fat milk, low fat cheeses.
Oils high in monounsaturates	Olive oil and canola oil.
Oils high in polyunsaturates	Corn oil, cottonseed oil, safflower oil, sesame oil, soybean oil, sunflower oil, walnut oil.

Stop

The red light signals stop — extreme danger ahead. These foods or products made with these foods will significantly increase the risk to your health.

FOOD	INCLUDES
Animal fats, tropical oils and processed oils	Butter, chicken fat, cocoa butter (chocolate), coconut oil, hydrogenated vegetable oils, lard, margarine, mayonnaise, palm oil, shortening.
Meats	Fatty meats, organ meats, processed meats.
Whole dairy	Cheese, cream, cream cheese, half-and-half, ice cream, milk, sour cream, yoghurt.
Nuts	Cashews, coconuts, macadamia nuts.
Salt products	Table salt, sea salt and ''lite'' salt.
Miscellaneous	Egg yolks, fried foods, nondairy creamers, nondairy whipped toppings, saccharin, caffeinated beverages.

DELICACIES FROM THE EAST

Eastern recipes adapt very easily to Pritikin-style cooking because traditional dishes often start with a basis of rice, use a sauce made mostly from fruits, vegetables and spices, and add only small quantities of animal protein (meat, fish or chicken) as a delicious garnish.

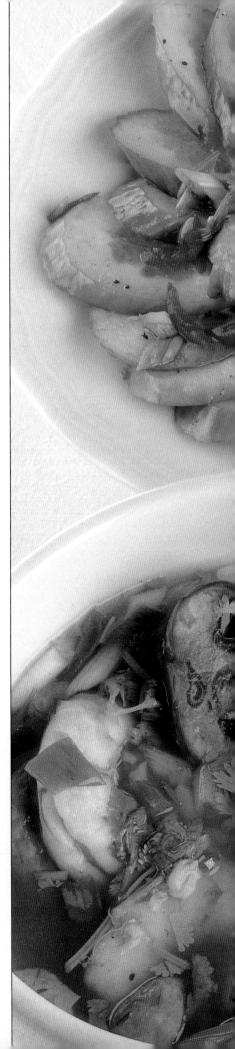

FIERY FOOD FROM THAILAND

Thai food is one of the world's hottest cuisines, so if you prefer milder food, use less than the recommended quantity of chillies. If a sauce is too hot, never gulp down iced water; it is better to munch on a lime or lemon wedge, or have some skim milk or yoghurt. To minimise the 'heat', remove seeds from chillies before using them, but be very careful not to touch your eyes when cutting chillies.

Although you can use substitutes for some ingredients, it is worth searching for authentic Thai herbs and spices. Most Asian food stores stock imported and locally produced ingredients. Never substitute parsley for fresh coriander — this gives Thai cuisine its quintessential flavour.

SPICY SOUR PRAWN SOUP

500 g (1 lb) fresh green (uncooked) prawns
7 cups water
2 stalks lemon grass, tender part only, finely chopped
3 Kaffir lime leaves
1 tablespoon fish sauce
4 fresh red or green chillies, finely sliced
100 g (3½ oz) button mushrooms, halved
3 tablespoons fresh lemon or lime juice
GARNISH
1 bunch fresh coriander leaves, roughly chopped
4 shallots, chopped

Shell and devein prawns but leave tails intact. Rinse prawn heads and crush slightly. Bring water to the boil. Add prawn heads, lemon grass, lime leaves, fish sauce and chillies. Boil for 2 minutes then reduce heat and simmer slowly for 10 minutes. Strain through a fine sieve.

Add prawns, mushrooms and lemon juice. Bring to the boil then immediately reduce heat and simmer for 3 minutes only. Swirl through coriander and shallots and serve.

Serves 4–6

Spicy Sour Prawn Soup, Cucumber Salad and Grilled Coriander and Garlic Chicken

CUCUMBER SALAD

1 medium-sized cucumber, peeled, seeded and finely diced
1 fresh red chilli, finely sliced
3 shallots, finely sliced
1 tablespoon fresh lemon juice
1 tablespoon salt-reduced soy sauce
2 teaspoons vinegar
freshly ground black pepper
fresh chopped coriander leaves, for garnish

Combine first seven ingredients. Garnish with coriander leaves and serve.

Serves 4–6

GRILLED CORIANDER AND GARLIC CHICKEN

1 kg (2 lb 2 oz) chicken pieces, skinned
fresh coriander sprigs, for garnish

MARINADE
12 cloves garlic
2 bunches fresh coriander
2 teaspoons freshly ground pepper
2 fresh red chillies
1 tablespoon lemon juice

Blend marinade ingredients and rub over chicken pieces. Refrigerate overnight or for at least 3 hours. Grill or barbecue chicken pieces. Garnish with coriander and serve.

Serves 4–6

CHICKEN AND MUSHROOM SOUP

3 cloves garlic, finely chopped
1 tablespoon finely chopped fresh coriander
1 teaspoon freshly ground black pepper
6 cups defatted chicken stock (see recipe)
500 g (1 lb) diced uncooked chicken fillets
1 tablespoon fish sauce
125 g button mushrooms, halved
4 finely chopped shallots, for garnish

Combine garlic, coriander and pepper. Dry-fry in a large saucepan for 1–2 minutes. Add all ingredients except shallots and bring to the boil. Reduce heat and simmer for 10–12 minutes. Garnish with shallots and serve.

Serves 4–6

Hot Red Beef Curry

HOT RED BEEF CURRY

This is one of my favourite curries. It is fiery, but delicious!

1 kg (2 lb 2 oz) topside beef, trimmed of all visible fat and diced
2 cups defatted beef, chicken or vegetable stock (see recipe)
2 teaspoons cornflour
1 tablespoon fish sauce

RED CURRY PASTE
8 fresh red chillies (including seeds)
2 stalks of lemon grass, tender part only
¼ cup chopped fresh coriander
4 shallots, chopped
4 cloves garlic
1 tablespoon chopped fresh ginger root
freshly ground black pepper

To make curry paste, blend or pound ingredients until well mashed. Preheat non-stick frypan. Saute diced beef for 5 minutes and set aside. Pour in ¼ cup stock and bring to the boil. Add curry paste, reduce heat and simmer uncovered for 2 minutes. Mix remaining 1¾ cups stock with cornflour. Add to pan with beef and fish sauce. Cover and simmer slowly for 1 hour until beef is tender.

Before serving, reduce excess liquid by simmering uncovered for 10–15 minutes. Allow curry to stand for at least 1 hour before serving. (It tastes even better the next day!) Serve with brown rice.

Serves 4–6

STEAMED FISH WITH GINGER SAUCE

1 kg (2 lb 2 oz) fish fillets or 1 whole fish
fresh chopped coriander leaves, for garnish

GINGER SAUCE
1 tablespoon chopped fresh ginger root
1 teaspoon vinegar
2 tablespoons salt-reduced soy sauce
1 tablespoon fish sauce
2 cloves garlic, chopped
4 shallots, chopped
1 tablespoon cornflour mixed with ½ cup water
1 tablespoon fresh orange or apple juice

Blend together all sauce ingredients and place in a saucepan. Simmer, stirring, until sauce reaches boiling point. Reduce heat, simmer and stir for another minute.

Steam fish for about 8 minutes, until flesh is white and flakes. Pour ginger sauce over fish. Garnish with coriander and serve with brown rice.

Serves 4–6

CHILLI CHICKEN WITH BASIL

1 cup defatted chicken stock (see recipe)
4 cloves garlic, finely chopped
3 fresh red chillies, finely chopped
1 kg (2 lb 2 oz) chicken pieces, skinned and chopped into bite-sized pieces
1 cup chopped fresh basil leaves
1 tablespoon fish sauce
juice 1 lemon

Bring chicken stock to the boil in a non-stick frypan. Add garlic and chillies and saute for 1 minute. Add the chicken pieces. Cover and simmer on a low heat for 40 minutes. Stir in the basil leaves and fish sauce. Heat through. Sprinkle with lemon juice and serve.

Serves 4–6

PRAWN SALAD

1 kg (2 lb 2 oz) prawns, tails left intact
1 small green capsicum, seeded and diced
1 tomato, seeded and diced
1 small white onion, diced
½ cucumber, peeled, seeded and diced
2 chopped shallots, for garnish

DRESSING
1 teaspoon vinegar
1 tablespoon fish sauce
juice 1 lime
juice 1 lemon
2 cloves garlic, chopped
1 tablespoon finely chopped fresh coriander
freshly ground black pepper

Place salad ingredients in a bowl. Combine dressing ingredients and pour over salad. Garnish with shallots and serve.

Serves 4–6

GRILLED FISH WITH CHILLI SAUCE

1 whole fish, rinsed, patted dry and scored on both sides

CHILLI SAUCE
5 fresh red chillies, chopped
1 tablespoon fish sauce
4 cloves garlic, finely chopped
1 tablespoon finely chopped fresh ginger root
juice 1 orange
juice 1 lime
1 tablespoon chopped fresh coriander
½ cup water mixed with 2 teaspoons cornflour

Preheat griller to high. Cook fish on both sides and set aside. Keep warm.

To make the chilli sauce, blend all sauce ingredients. Stir in water and cornflour mix and bring to the boil. Reduce heat and simmer, stirring, for 3 minutes. Pour sauce over fish and serve with brown rice.

Serves 4–6

SEAFOOD WITH BASIL AND MINT

1 kg (2 lb 2 oz) mixed seafood (fish fillets, prawns, calamari rings)
1 cup water
1 white onion, roughly chopped
2 cloves garlic, chopped
2 fresh red chillies, chopped
2 stalks lemon grass; tender part only, finely chopped
2 tablespoons fish sauce
1 tablespoon fresh lime juice
½ cup chopped fresh basil leaves
½ cup chopped fresh mint leaves
1 tablespoon finely chopped fresh coriander leaves

Chop fish fillets into small chunks; shell and devein prawns, leaving tails intact. Set aside. Bring water to the boil in large non-stick frypan. Add onion, garlic, chillies and lemon grass. Cover and simmer for 5 minutes. Add the mixed seafood, cover and simmer for 6–8 minutes. Combine fish sauce with lime juice, basil, mint and coriander. Lightly stir into frypan, heat through and serve with brown rice.

Serves 4–6

SATAYS

Traditionally, satays are served with peanut sauce but all nuts, except chestnuts, are excluded from the Pritikin eating plan. Vegetarians can substitute tofu or vegetables for chicken, beef or seafood.

500 g (1 lb) beef fillet or 500 g (1 lb) chicken fillet or 500 g (1 lb) mixed seafood pieces

MARINADE
**4 fresh red or green chillies, chopped
5 cloves garlic, chopped
1 stalk lemon grass, tender part only
1 teaspoon ground turmeric
1 tablespoon fish sauce
2 teaspoons finely chopped fresh ginger root
juice 1 lime
juice 1 orange
½ cup low-fat yoghurt
1 tablespoon finely chopped fresh coriander
freshly ground black pepper**

Remove all visible fat from beef or chicken and cut into small chunks.

To make the marinade, combine all ingredients and blend. Marinate beef, chicken or seafood in satay marinade in the refrigerator for at least 2 hours.

Thread satays onto metal or pre-soaked bamboo skewers. Preheat griller to high and cook satays for 2–3 minutes each side. Satays can also be barbecued.

Serves 4–6

MASSAMAN VEGETABLE CURRY

**12 dried red chillies
1 tablespoon coriander seeds
1 tablespoon cumin seeds
3 cardamom pods
2 whole cloves
½ teaspoon freshly grated nutmeg
1 teaspoon whole peppercorns
1 small stick cinnamon
2 cups water
5 cloves garlic, finely chopped
2 stalks lemon grass; tender part only, finely chopped
2 medium-sized white onions, finely sliced
500 g (1 lb) potatoes, peeled
500 g (1 lb) mixed vegetables (carrots, cauliflower, pumpkin, broccoli), chopped
2 tablespoons fish sauce
1 tablespoon vinegar
1 cup low-fat yoghurt**

Grind first 8 ingredients (spices) until powdered. Dry-fry in non-stick frypan until they are smoking vigorously. Remove spices and set aside.

Bring ½ cup water to the boil and add chopped garlic, lemon grass and onions. Reduce heat, cover and simmer for 5 minutes. Add ground spices and simmer, stirring, for 1 minute.

Combine vegetables, fish sauce and vinegar with remaining 1½ cups water and add to pan. Bring to the boil. Reduce heat, cover and simmer slowly for 40 minutes. Stir in yoghurt and serve with brown rice.

Serves 4–6

Satays served on a bed of lettuce

Massaman Vegetable Curry

HOT GREEN FISH CURRY

2 teaspoons ground coriander
2 teaspoons ground cumin
1 teaspoon ground nutmeg
1 teaspoon finely ground pepper
8 fresh green chillies, chopped
4 cloves garlic, chopped
1 stalk lemon grass, tender part only
**1 tablespoon chopped fresh
    coriander**
2 shallots, chopped
1 teaspoon lemon zest
1 teaspoon fresh lime juice
½ cup water
**1 tablespoon dried galangal, chopped
    (see Note)**
2 teaspoons cornflour
**1 kg (2 lb 2 oz) fish fillets, cut into
    small chunks**
**1–2 uncooked fresh prawns, shelled,
    deveined and chopped**

Preheat non-stick frypan and dry-fry first
four ingredients until they start to smoke.
Remove from pan. Puree chillies, garlic,
lemon grass, coriander, shallots, lemon
zest and lime juice. Combine this mixture
with ground spices and mash to a paste.

Bring ¼ cup water to the boil. Add
curry paste and galangal. Cover and
simmer 2–3 minutes.

Mix cornflour with remaining water and
add to pan, with all remaining
ingredients. Stir until well combined and
simmer uncovered for 15 minutes. Serve
with brown rice.

Note: Galangal is an aromatic herb with
a gingery-peppery taste.

Serves 4–6

THAI FISH CAKES

Traditionally, Thai fish cakes are deep-
fried, but these are cooked in a non-stick
frypan. They taste the same, but they're
not greasy.

**500 g (1 lb) uncooked fish fillets,
    roughly chopped (select fish which
    has few bones)**
3 tablespoons low-fat yoghurt
1 tablespoon fish sauce
**100 g (3½ oz) fresh green beans,
    trimmed and chopped**
**1 stalk lemon grass, tender part
    chopped**
**1 tablespoon green capsicum,
    seeded and chopped**
1 tablespoon cornflour
2 cloves fresh garlic, chopped
**2–3 fresh red or green chillies,
    chopped**
**2 teaspoons chopped fresh coriander
    leaves**
1 egg white

Place all ingredients in a blender for a few
seconds only, or mash to a fine paste.
Chill in refrigerator overnight or for at
least 2 hours.

Form mixture into small, flat fish cakes.
Preheat non-stick frypan to very hot and
cook fish cakes for 2–3 minutes each
side until brown. Serve with a sweet and
sour dipping sauce or lemon wedges.

Makes 18–20 fish cakes

A TASTE OF JAPAN

The Japanese are the longest living race on earth. Their diet is naturally healthy but you may wish to cut back further, by reducing salty ingredients such as soy sauce, dried bonito fish flakes, miso paste and dried seaweed.

A Japanese meal usually begins with a clear seafood or vegetable soup. During the meal it is common to serve a heartier miso soup. Main course dishes include small pieces of marinated grilled chicken or fish, accompanied by rice and vegetables, and followed by green tea and fresh fruit.

There is a great emphasis on presentation. Japanese food is more than sustenance — it is an art form, so get out your best porcelain, arrange some flowers and enjoy your Pritikin-style Japanese cuisine.

SUSHI RICE

3 cups brown rice
4 cups water
3 tablespoons rice vinegar
2 tablespoons apple juice
concentrate

Thoroughly rinse rice. Bring all ingredients to the boil. Reduce heat, cover and simmer on a low heat for 40 minutes. Allow to cool.

Serves 4–6

CUCUMBER ROLL

3 sheets nori (dried seaweed) cut in half
sushi rice (see recipe)
½ cucumber, seeded and cut into thin strips
salt-reduced soy sauce

Place one half-sheet nori on a bamboo sushi mat. Spread small amount of rice over first half of nori sheet. Top with cucumber strips, and sprinkle with a few drops of salt-reduced soy sauce. Carefully roll up tightly. Cut roll into short lengths. Repeat with remaining nori sheets. Serve with a dipping sauce of salt-reduced soy sauce.

Serves 4–6

Nigiri Sushi and Cucumber Roll

TUNA ROLL

3 sheets nori (dried seaweed) cut in half
sushi rice (see recipe)
fresh tuna, sliced into thin strips
salt-reduced soy sauce

Place one half-sheet nori on a bamboo sushi mat. Spread first half of nori sheet with thin layer of rice. Top with tuna strips and a few drops of salt-reduced soy sauce. Roll up tightly and cut into short lengths. Repeat with remaining nori sheets.

Serves 4–6

NIGIRI SUSHI

fresh seafood pieces (garfish, ocean perch, squid, salmon, prawns)
sushi rice (see recipe)
fresh parsley and shallots, for garnish

MARINADE
¼ cup dashi (see recipe)
2 tablespoons mirin (see *Note*)
2 teaspoons rice vinegar

Cut seafood pieces into thin slices and marinate for 30 minutes. Take small amount of sushi rice and shape into small oval shapes. Top with marinated seafood pieces and arrange decoratively on a plate or wooden board. Garnish with parsley and shallots and serve.

Note: Mirin is a Japanese rice wine, available at Japanese and some Asian food stores. If unavailable, substitute sherry, but the flavour will be different.

Serves 4–6

CHICKEN AND VEGETABLE SOUP

3 dried shitake mushrooms
6 cups dashi (see recipe)
3 shallots, finely chopped
1 chicken fillet, thinly sliced
1 stalk celery, finely diced
1 small carrot, cut into thin strips

Soak mushrooms in hot water for 30 minutes. Remove from water. Cut off stalks and cut mushrooms into thin slices. Bring dashi to the boil and add all other ingredients. Reduce heat and simmer on a low heat for 8 minutes.

Serves 4–6

TOFU AND NOODLE SOUP

**100 g (3½ oz) soba buckwheat
  noodles**
½ cup mirin (rice wine)
½ cup salt-reduced soy sauce
300 g (9½ oz) fresh tofu, diced
6 cups dashi (see recipe)
3 shallots, finely chopped

Bring a large saucepan of water to the
boil. Plunge in noodles and cook until
tender. Drain and set aside.
   Bring mirin and soy sauce to the boil.
Add diced tofu, reduce heat and simmer
for 4 minutes. Add noodles and dashi
and heat through. Sprinkle with shallots
and serve.

Serves 4–6

*Tofu and Noodle Soup with Vegetarian
Tempura*

MISO SOUP

2 dried shitake mushrooms (see *Note*)
6 cups dashi (see recipe)
2 tablespoons low-salt miso paste
2 tablespoons grated carrot
3 shallots, finely chopped

Soak mushrooms in hot water for 30
minutes. Drain, trim off stalks and slice.
Bring dashi to the boil. Immediately
remove from heat. Mix one cup of dashi
with.miso paste. Return to saucepan and
add mushrooms and grated carrot.
Simmer for 2 minutes. Sprinkle with
shallots and serve.

Note: These dark brown mushrooms are
a staple ingredient in Japanese cooking.
They are available in dried form from
Asian food stores.

Serves 4–6

DASHI

Dashi is a stock used in many Japanese
recipes. It is made with dried sea kelp
(kombu) and dried bonito fish flakes,
available in Asian and some health food
stores. Dashi is essential if you want your
Japanese recipes to have an authentic
flavour.

40 g (1½ oz) kombu
6 cups water
½ cup bonito fish flakes

Rinse kombu in cold water. Add to water
in a saucepan and bring slowly to the
boil. Just before water reaches boiling
point, remove from heat and discard
kombu. Return water to heat and add
bonito flakes. Bring to the boil.
Immediately remove from heat and let the
flakes settle in the bottom of the pan.
Strain the dashi through a sieve and use
for soups, sautes and sauces.

Serves 4–6

CHICKEN YAKITORI

600 g (1¼ lb) chicken fillets, trimmed of all visible fat
½ cup salt-reduced soy sauce
½ cup mirin (rice wine)
squeeze lemon juice
1 teaspoon finely grated fresh ginger root

Cut the chicken into small pieces and thread onto metal or pre-soaked bamboo skewers. Mix together soy sauce, mirin, lemon juice and ginger. Place in a small saucepan and bring to the boil. Immediately remove from the heat and allow to cool. Leave chicken in this marinade for 30 minutes.

Preheat griller to high. Cook chicken on both sides for several minutes until tender. Baste during cooking. Serve with brown rice.

Serves 4–6

VEGETARIAN TEMPURA

500 g (1 lb) mixed vegetables (pumpkin, leeks, broccoli, eggplant, capsicum, carrot)
lemon wedges, for garnish

BATTER
1 egg white
1 cup iced water
1 cup wholemeal flour
¼ teaspoon baking powder

Preheat oven to 200°C (400°F). Slice vegetables thinly. Break broccoli into florets.

Mix batter ingredients. Dip in vegetable pieces and place on non-stick baking tray. Bake for 15–20 minutes until brown. Serve with dipping sauce of salt-reduced soy and lemon wedges.

Serves 4–6

COLD NOODLES WITH NORI

1 cup dashi (see recipe)
¼ cup salt-reduced soy sauce
1 tablespoon grated fresh ginger root
½ cup mirin (rice wine)
1 tablespoon bonito flakes
200 g (6½ oz) soba buckwheat noodles
3 sheets nori (dried seaweed)
4 shallots, finely chopped

Combine dashi, soy sauce, ginger, mirin and bonito flakes. Bring almost to the boil and strain through a sieve. Allow to cool.

Bring large saucepan of water to the boil and add noodles. Cook until tender. Drain and rinse under cold running water. Place noodles in individual serving bowls with 1–2 ice cubes in each.

Toast nori under griller. Crumble toasted nori over the noodles. Pour sauce over noodles. Garnish with shallots and serve.

Serves 4–6

CHICKEN WITH RICE

225 g (8 oz) chicken fillets trimmed of all visible fat
1 cup dashi (see recipe)
¼ cup sake
¼ cup salt-reduced soy sauce
4 cups cooked brown rice
4 egg whites, lightly beaten
4 shallots, cut into short lengths

Cut the chicken into thin slices. Bring dashi to the boil and add sake and soy sauce. Add chicken, reduce heat and simmer for 5 minutes. Pour in lightly beaten egg whites and simmer for another 1–2 minutes.

Place 1 cup rice into each bowl. Top with chicken and sauce and sprinkle with chopped shallots.

Serves 4

SPINACH SALAD

6 spinach leaves

DRESSING
¼ cup salt-reduced soy sauce
1 tablespoon dried bonito flakes
2 teaspoons toasted sesame seeds
squeeze lemon juice

Remove centre stalk of spinach leaves. Blanch leaves for 1 minute in boiling water. Remove and drain. Chop into pieces. Combine dressing ingredients and pour over spinach. Chill and serve.

Serves 4–6

SEAWEED SALAD

45 g (1½ oz) dried wakame seaweed
chopped shallots, for garnish

DRESSING
1 tablespoon toasted sesame seeds
2 tablespoons low-salt miso paste (bean paste)
1 tablespoon rice vinegar

Rinse wakame thoroughly under cold water. Then soak, covered in warm water, for 15 minutes. Rinse again and drain thoroughly. Chop into short lengths.

Combine dressing ingredients and pour over wakame. Garnish with shallots and serve.

Serves 4–6

SHABU SHABU

Shabu Shabu is similar to Mongolian Hot Pot. An array of fresh ingredients — beef, chicken or seafood, vegetables and noodles — is cooked at the table by each individual.

8 shitake mushrooms
1 kg (2 lb 2 oz) fillet steak, trimmed of all visible fat
8 cups defatted chicken stock (see recipe)
1 small Chinese cabbage, shredded
8 shallots, cut into short lengths
2 carrots, sliced
200 g (6½ oz) soba buckwheat noodles
400 g (12½ oz) fresh tofu, diced

DIPPING SAUCE
½ cup salt-reduced soy sauce
1 tablespoon rice vinegar
1 tablespoon sake
½ cup dashi (see recipe)
1 teaspoon grated fresh ginger root

Combine all sauce ingredients and pour into individual bowls. Soak mushrooms for 30 minutes in hot water. Trim off stalks and slice. Cut the meat into thin slices. (You can partially freeze the meat for about 10 minutes to make it easier to slice thinly.)

Pour stock into electric frypan and bring to the boil. Reduce heat and allow liquid to simmer. Each guest then cooks his portion of meat, vegetables, noodles and tofu. The delicious cooked morsels are then placed in the dipping sauce. Serve with a large bowl of cooked brown rice.

Serves 4–6

GRILLED GARFISH

6 medium-sized garfish
½ cup mirin (rice wine)
2 tablespoons salt-reduced soy sauce
1 teaspoon finely grated fresh ginger root

Marinate garfish in mirin, soy sauce and ginger root for 30 minutes. Preheat griller to high and cook for 15 minutes. Garnish with lemon wedges and cucumber slices.

Serves 6

PRAWN TEMPURA

1 kg fresh uncooked large prawns, shelled and deveined, leaving tails on

BATTER
2 egg whites
2 cups iced water
2 cups wholemeal flour
½ teaspoon baking powder

TO SERVE
salt-reduced soy sauce
lemon wedges

Mix batter ingredients. Dip in prawns and place on non-stick baking tray. Bake for 15–20 minutes until brown. Serve with dipping sauce of salt-reduced soy sauce and lemon wedges.

Serves 4–6

BEEF TERIYAKI

4 small fillet steaks, trimmed of any visible fat
¼ cup salt-reduced soy sauce
¼ cup mirin (rice wine)
1 teaspoon finely chopped fresh ginger root

Combine all ingredients. Marinate for 30 minutes. Fry in non-stick frypan or grill until tender.

Serves 4

CHICKEN TONKATSU

This dish is traditionally made with pork, but lean beef or chicken can be used instead.

4 chicken breasts, trimmed of all visible fat and halved
½ cup salt-reduced soy sauce
1 tablespoon mirin (rice wine)
freshly ground black pepper
1 cup wholemeal flour
2 egg whites, lightly beaten
1 cup homemade Pritikin breadcrumbs
lemon wedges, for garnish
extra salt-reduced soy sauce, for dipping

Marinate chicken breasts in soy sauce, mirin and pepper for 1 hour. Drain, and dip in flour and egg white. Roll in breadcrumbs, pressing firmly. Chill in refrigerator for 30 minutes or in freezer for 10 minutes. Preheat oven to 190°C (375°F).

Bake for 30 minutes. Slice into thick strips, garnish with lemon wedges and serve with soy sauce for dipping.

Serves 4–6

MUSHROOM SALAD

12 shitake mushrooms
½ cup grated white daikon radish
¼ cup salt-reduced soy sauce
1 teaspoon finely grated fresh ginger root
2 teaspoons rice vinegar

Soak mushrooms in hot water for 30 minutes. Remove from water. Discard stalks and slice mushrooms. Combine all ingredients. Marinate for 30 minutes and serve.

Serves 4

Chicken Tonkatsu

AROMATIC DISHES FROM INDIA

Indian cuisine varies enormously, and while much of the food is aromatic, the flavours are often mild.

India is a vegetarian's delight. Meat, fish and chicken are eaten in small quantities and the diet is largely vegetables, rice, bread and milk products. Authentic Indian cooks grind their own fresh spices, regarding commercially prepared curry powder with disdain. You can make up your own curry powders by grinding spices quickly and easily in a coffee grinder. Dry-fry them in a preheated non-stick frying pan before adding them to the cooking pot.

Indian food improves with age; the flavours intensify, so don't throw out any leftovers.

TANDOORI CHICKEN

This is one of India's most celebrated dishes. Traditionally, it is cooked in a tandoor, or clay oven, which gives the chicken a very special, slightly smoky flavour. However, you can produce a delicious result in your own oven. This recipe can be used for meat or seafood, and I strongly recommend you use freshly ground spices to create a genuine tandoori paste. Tandoori chicken can also be cooked on the barbecue.

1.5 kg (3 lb) chicken pieces, on the bone
1 tablespoon vinegar
1 cup low-fat yoghurt
lemon wedges, for garnish

TANDOORI PASTE
3 fresh red chillies
1 onion
6 cloves garlic
1 tablespoon chopped fresh ginger root
2 tablespoons lemon juice
1 teaspoon ground cumin
1 teaspoon freshly ground black pepper
2 teaspoons ground coriander
2 whole cloves
small piece cinnamon stick
1 bay leaf
dash turmeric
dash nutmeg
1 teaspoon paprika

Remove all skin from chicken and prick pieces with a fork. To make tandoori paste, puree chillies, onion, garlic, ginger and lemon juice. Place in a bowl. Preheat non-stick frypan and dry-fry remaining tandoori paste spices until smoking vigorously. Combine with the puree and mix to form a paste.

Rub this paste thoroughly into chicken pieces. Sprinkle over vinegar and pour over yoghurt. Combine well and marinate in refrigerator for at least 24 hours. Stir mixture occasionally.

Preheat oven to 190°C (375°F). Place chicken pieces on rack in roasting pan. Bake for 35–40 minutes until tender. Baste during cooking process with any remaining marinade. Garnish with lemon wedges and serve with salad and wholemeal chapatis (see recipe).

Note: Tandoori Chicken can also be grilled instead of roasted.

Serves 4–6

CAULIFLOWER WITH YOGHURT

1 small cauliflower, divided into florets
½ teaspoon turmeric
freshly ground black pepper
2 teaspoons mustard seeds
1½ cups low-fat yoghurt
1 teaspoon finely chopped fresh ginger root
2 garlic cloves, finely chopped
½ fresh red or green chilli, finely chopped

Steam or boil cauliflower until tender. Drain and set aside. Preheat non-stick frypan and dry-fry turmeric, pepper and mustard seeds. When seeds begin to pop, add to yoghurt. Stir in ginger, garlic and chilli. Add cauliflower florets and mix well. Refrigerate for 1 hour and serve.

Serves 4–6

Tandoori Chicken served with salad and Wholemeal Chapatis

KITCHERI

2 cups brown rice
2 cups red lentils
5 cups water
1 large onion, sliced
2 cloves garlic, finely chopped
1 teaspoon finely chopped fresh
**   ginger root**
2 cardamom pods, slightly bruised
small piece cinnamon stick
1 whole clove
½ teaspoon turmeric
1 teaspoon cumin seeds
1 fresh red or green chilli, finely
**   chopped**

Rinse rice and lentils, drain and set aside.
Bring 1 cup water to the boil and add
onion, garlic and ginger. Reduce heat,
cover and simmer for 5 minutes. Add rice
and lentils to the pan and set aside.

In a non-stick frypan dry-fry cardamom
pods, cinnamon stick, clove, turmeric,
and cumin seeds. Remove when
smoking. Reserve the cumin seeds. Add
remaining spices and chilli to rice and
lentil mixture.

Pour in remaining 4 cups water and
bring to the boil. Reduce heat, cover and
simmer for 45 minutes. Sprinkle with
cumin seeds and serve with
accompaniments — chutney, low-fat
yoghurt, fresh fruit pieces — or with Beef
Koftas (see recipe).

Serves 4–6

PAKORAS

800 g (1½ lb) mixed vegetables
**   (broccoli, cauliflower, capsicum,**
**   eggplant, onions, potato, pumpkin)**

BATTER
2 cups wholemeal or besan (chick
**   pea) flour**
½ teaspoon baking powder
2 cups water
2 egg whites, lightly beaten
½ teaspoon ground turmeric
1 teaspoon cumin seeds
freshly ground black pepper

Preheat oven to 190°C (375°F). Chop
vegetables into bite-sized pieces and set
aside.

To make batter, sift flour and baking
powder. Add water and combine well.
Add all other batter ingredients. Dip in
vegetable pieces and place on non-stick
baking tray. Bake for 25 minutes until
brown. Serve with low-fat yoghurt or
chutney dip.

Serves 4–6

BEEF KOFTAS

1 kg (2 lb 2 oz) lean minced topside
**   beef**
2 fresh red chillies, pureed
2 fresh green chillies, pureed
3 cloves garlic, pureed
freshly ground black pepper
2 egg whites, lightly beaten
1 tablespoon wholemeal flour
1 tablespoon vinegar
½ cup chopped fresh coriander

CURRY SAUCE
¾ cup water
2 onions, finely chopped
1 tablespoon finely chopped fresh
**   ginger root**
½ teaspoon ground turmeric
2 teaspoons freshly ground coriander
1 teaspoon ground cumin
½ cup low-fat yoghurt

Mix together beef, chillies, garlic, pepper
and egg whites. Form into small balls,
sprinkle with flour and set aside.

To make curry sauce, bring ½ cup
water to the boil. Add onions and ginger.
Reduce heat, cover and simmer for 5
minutes. Set aside. Dry-fry turmeric,
ground coriander and cumin until
smoking. Add to onion and ginger
mixture with yoghurt and remaining ¼
cup water.

Add meatballs, cover and simmer on
low heat for 35–40 minutes. Add vinegar
and chopped fresh coriander and
combine well. Heat through and serve.
Kitcheri is a delicious accompaniment to
this dish (see recipe).

Serves 4–6

Kitcheri and Beef Koftas

Vegetable Samosas

DHAL

2½ cups red lentils
6 cups water
5 cloves garlic, finely chopped
2.5 cm (1 in) piece cinnamon stick
6 black peppercorns
8 cardamom pods, slightly bruised
2 teaspoons turmeric
3 teaspoons cumin seeds

Wash lentils in colander. Discard any that float to the surface. Place lentils in a heavy-based saucepan with water and all ingredients except cumin seeds. Bring to the boil. Reduce heat, cover and simmer for 45–60 minutes. Stir at regular intervals. If mixture becomes too thick, add a little more water. The consistency can vary according to your preference for a thick or thin dhal.

Allow to cool. Remove cardamom pods, peppercorns and cinnamon stick. For a smoother texture, blend or mash lentils. Just before serving, heat a non-stick frypan and dry-fry cumin seeds until they start to smoke. Sprinkle heated cumin seeds over dhal. Serve with curry and brown rice.

Serves 4–6

VEGETABLE SAMOSAS

1½ cups wholemeal flour
pinch baking powder
½ cup water
1½ tablespoons skim milk
lemon wedges and chutney, for garnish

SAMOSA FILLING
3–4 potatoes (about 800 g), peeled and chopped
¾ cup water
1 large onion, finely sliced
2 cloves garlic, finely chopped
1 cup fresh or frozen peas
1 small carrot, grated
1 teaspoon finely chopped fresh ginger root
1 teaspoon ground cumin
½ teaspoon ground coriander
½ teaspoon ground turmeric
freshly ground black pepper
1 fresh green chilli, finely chopped or blended
½ cup finely chopped fresh coriander
2 tablespoons lemon juice

To make dough, sift flour and baking powder. Add water and milk, combine and knead for 10 minutes. Wrap in plastic and set aside.

To make filling, steam or boil the potatoes, and mash. Bring water to the boil. Add onion and garlic. Reduce heat, cover and simmer for 5 minutes. Add peas, carrot and ginger. Cover and simmer for 5 minutes. Drain well. Combine with mashed potato and mix thoroughly.

Preheat non-stick frypan and dry-fry cumin, ground coriander, turmeric and pepper until they smoke. Add to filling mixture with chilli, fresh coriander and lemon juice. Mix well and allow to cool.

Preheat oven to 190°C (375°F). Take small amounts of dough and form into balls. Roll these out into very thin circular pancakes. Cut pancakes in half. Place 1½ teaspoons of filling on one side of half pancake. Fold over to form a triangular shape. Seal edges and brush top with extra skim milk. Bake for 25 minutes until brown. Garnish with lemon wedges and chutney and serve.

Note: Instead of cutting circular pancakes in half, you can form pastie shapes. For a crowd, I sometimes make one large pastie and serve the samosas in thick strips. (If there is any samosa mixture over, form into balls, brush with egg white and bake in the oven — easy Indian rissoles!)

Serves 4–6

PRAWN CURRY

1 kg (2 lb 2 oz) fresh uncooked
   prawns, shelled and deveined;
   leave tails on
½ cup water or stock
2 large white onions, finely sliced
lemon wedges, for garnish

CURRY MARINADE
1 teaspoon ground turmeric
2 tablespoons ground coriander
4 cardamom pods, ground
freshly ground black pepper
1 tablespoon finely chopped fresh
   ginger root
4 garlic cloves, finely chopped
3 fresh red or green chillies
¼ cup brown vinegar
1 tablespoon fresh tomato paste,
   mixed with 1 tablespoon water
1 bunch fresh coriander, finely
   chopped

Preheat non-stick frypan. Dry-fry
turmeric, coriander, cardamom and
pepper until heated through and
smoking. Remove from frypan and mix
with other curry marinade ingredients.
Marinate prawns in marinade for at least
1 hour — preferably overnight.

Bring water to the boil and add onion.
Reduce heat, cover and simmer for 10
minutes. Add prawns with marinade and
simmer for 5–10 minutes. Garnish with
lemon wedges and serve with brown
rice.

Serves 4–6

FAVOURITE FISH CURRY

This is a 'wet' curry and the delicious
gravy is poured over rice.

1 teaspoon ground turmeric
1 tablespoon ground coriander
2 teaspoons ground cumin seeds
freshly ground black pepper
1½ cups water
2 large white onions, finely sliced
4 cloves garlic, finely chopped
2 teaspoons finely chopped fresh
   ginger root
2 fresh red or green chillies, chopped
2 large very ripe tomatoes, roughly
   chopped
1 teaspoon tomato paste
1 kg (2 lb 2 oz) firm fish fillets,
   chopped into thick slices
½ cup chopped fresh coriander
lemon wedges, for garnish

Preheat non-stick frypan. Dry-fry
turmeric, coriander, cumin and pepper
until they are heated through and
smoking. Remove from heat and set
aside.

Pour 1 cup water into pan. Bring to the
boil and add onions, garlic, ginger and
chillies. Reduce heat, cover and simmer
for 5 minutes. Add the spices, tomato
pieces and tomato paste. Stir until well
combined, then cover and simmer for a
further 3 minutes.

Add fish pieces and remaining ½ cup
water. Gently stir until combined. Cover
and simmer on a low heat for 20 minutes.
Before serving, stir in chopped coriander.
Garnish with lemon wedges. Squeeze
juice over fish curry before eating. Serve
with brown rice and accompaniments.

Serves 4–6

TAJ MAHAL CHICKEN

1¼ cups defatted chicken stock
   (see recipe)
2 large white onions, thinly sliced
2 fresh red or green chillies, finely
   chopped
4 cloves garlic, finely chopped
1 tablespoon finely chopped fresh
   ginger root
1.5 kg (3 lb) chicken pieces, skinned
1 cup low-fat yoghurt
1 cup finely chopped fresh coriander
2 tablespoons finely chopped fresh
   mint leaves

SPICES
2 cardamom pods
2 teaspoons ground turmeric
1 bay leaf
1 teaspoon black mustard seeds
1 teaspoon cumin seeds
1 small piece cinnamon stick
1 clove
3 peppercorns

Preheat non-stick frypan. Add spices and
dry-fry. Remove from heat when spices
smoke.

Bring 1 cup stock to the boil and add
onions. Reduce heat, cover and simmer
for 4 minutes. Add chillies, garlic and
ginger and cook for a further 2 minutes.
Stir in dry-fried spices until well
combined. Remove this spicy mixture
from frypan.

Add chicken pieces to frypan and
saute until lightly browned all over.
Combine all ingredients except coriander
and mint. Cover and simmer on a low
heat for 40 minutes. Stir in coriander and
mint and serve with brown rice.

Serves 4–6

PUNJAB POTATO PUREE

1 kg (2 lb 2 oz) potatoes, peeled and
   chopped
1 tablespoon black mustard seeds
1 teaspoon ground coriander
1 teaspoon ground cumin
freshly ground black pepper
½ cup water
1 onion, finely chopped
1 clove garlic, finely chopped
1 teaspoon finely chopped fresh
   ginger root
¼ cup low-fat yoghurt
1 fresh red or green chilli, finely
   chopped
½ cup finely chopped fresh coriander
lemon wedges and chopped fresh
   coriander, for garnish

Steam or boil potatoes until tender, and
reserve. Preheat non-stick frypan. Dry-fry
mustard seeds, coriander, cumin and
pepper until smoking and mustard seeds
pop; set aside.

Bring water to the boil. Add onion,
garlic and ginger. Reduce heat, cover
and simmer for 5 minutes. Drain and
combine with dry-fried spices.

Mash potatoes with yoghurt and add in
all other ingredients.

Garnish with lemon wedges and fresh
coriander.

Serves 4–6

RAJASTHANI RICE

3 cardamom pods, slightly bruised
1 small piece cinnamon stick
3 whole cloves
6 black peppercorns
3 cups brown rice, well rinsed and
   drained
1 teaspoon grated orange zest
1 teaspoon grated lemon zest
3 cups water
1 cup fresh orange juice
½ cup mixed dried fruit, rinsed under
   cold water and drained

Preheat non-stick frypan and dry-fry
cardamom, cinnamon, cloves and
peppercorns until they begin to smoke.
Add to rice with all ingredients except
dried fruit.

Stir until well combined and bring to
boil. Reduce heat, cover and simmer
slowly until cooked — about 40 minutes.
Mix through dried fruit and serve with
curry and accompaniments.

Serves 4–6

Rajasthani Rice

CARDAMOM FRUIT SALAD

1 cup chopped bananas
1 cup chopped peaches
1 cup grapes
1 cup chopped mangoes
1 cup chopped kiwi fruit
8 cardamom pods, seeds finely
  ground
1 cup low-fat yoghurt
¼ cup apple juice concentrate
fresh mint sprigs, for garnish

Combine all ingredients. Refrigerate for at least 2 hours or overnight. Garnish with mint and serve.　　　　Serves 4–6

RAITA

1 cucumber, peeled and thinly sliced
1 cup low-fat yoghurt
1 clove garlic, minced
pinch chilli powder
freshly ground black pepper

Combine all ingredients, chill and serve as a side dish for curries.

Serves 4–6

BANANAS WITH LEMON

4 bananas, sliced
juice 1 lemon
2 teaspoons grated lemon zest

Combine all ingredients, chill and serve as a side dish for curries.

Serves 4–6

HOT BEEF VINDALOO

**1.5 kg (3 lb) topside beef, trimmed of
  all visible fat and diced
1 cup defatted chicken stock
  (see recipe) or water
4 medium-sized white onions, finely
  sliced
3 fresh red or green chillies, finely
  chopped
5 cloves garlic, finely chopped
1 tablespoon finely chopped fresh
  ginger root**
CURRY PASTE
**1 teaspoon ground turmeric
1 tablespoon ground coriander
1 teaspoon ground peppercorns
1 teaspoon ground cumin
1 teaspoon ground fenugreek
¼ cup brown vinegar
1 tablespoon tomato paste**

To make curry paste, preheat non-stick
frypan and add ground spices. Heat
through; remove from heat when they are
smoking. Mix with vinegar and tomato
paste until smooth. Pour over meat and
marinate for at least 1 hour.

Bring ½ cup stock to the boil and add
onions. Reduce heat, cover and simmer
for 5 minutes. Add chillies, garlic and
ginger and cook a further 3 minutes.
Remove from frypan and set aside.

Add marinated meat and saute for 10
minutes. Add remaining stock. Cover and
simmer on a low heat for 1 hour, until
meat is tender. Serve with brown rice.

Serves 4–6

WHOLEMEAL CHAPATIS

**2½ cups wholemeal flour
1 cup water
1 tablespoon skim milk**

Sift flour and gradually add water and
milk. Combine well and knead for 10
minutes on a lightly floured board. Wrap
in plastic wrap or slightly damp cloth and
allow to stand for 2 hours.

Form small pieces of dough into balls
and roll out as thinly as a crepe. Preheat
non-stick frypan. Cook chapatis for 1
minute. Press edges with a cloth to make
the chapatis light and bubbly. Turn over
and cook for another minute.

Wrap cooked chapatis in clean tea
towel and serve with curries and chutney.

Serves 4–6

*Hot Beef Vindaloo served with rice and
Wholemeal Chapatis*

AVIYAL MIXED VEGETABLES

**2 fresh green chillies
1 onion
1 teaspoon grated fresh ginger root
2 cloves garlic
1 cup water
1 teaspoon cumin seeds
2 teaspoons black mustard seeds
½ teaspoon ground turmeric
freshly ground black pepper
1 kg (2 lb 2 oz) mixed vegetables
  (potatoes, carrots, beans,
  capsicum, broccoli, cauliflower)
1 cup low-fat yoghurt
½ cup finely chopped fresh coriander
lemon wedges, for garnish**

Puree chillies, onion, ginger and garlic. In
a casserole, bring water to the boil and
add pureed mixture. Cover, reduce heat
and simmer for 5 minutes. In a pan, dry-
fry cumin and black mustard seeds,
turmeric and pepper until seeds pop.
Add to casserole, cover and simmer for a
further 2 minutes.

Add potatoes only; cover and simmer
for 15 minutes. Then add other
vegetables; cover and simmer for 8–10
minutes. Stir in yoghurt and coriander.
Garnish with lemon wedges and serve.

Serves 4–6

PEAS AND BEANS IN SPICY TOMATO SAUCE

**1 onion
1 clove garlic
1 teaspoon grated fresh ginger root
1 fresh red chilli, chopped
¼ cup water
1 heaped teaspoon cumin seeds
1 teaspoon ground turmeric
freshly ground black pepper
3 very ripe tomatoes
2 tablespoons lemon juice
250 g (8 oz) fresh shelled peas
500 g (1 lb) snake or French beans,
  cut into short lengths**

Blend onion, garlic, ginger and chilli. Add
puree to a pan of boiling water. Cover,
reduce heat and simmer for 5 minutes.
Dry-fry cumin, turmeric and pepper. Add
to pan and cook for a further minute.
Puree tomatoes and lemon juice and add
to pan with peas and beans. Cover and
simmer for 10–12 minutes and serve.

Serves 4–6

BRAISED CABBAGE WITH CUMIN

**1¼ cups water
1 large onion, finely sliced
2 teaspoons finely chopped fresh
  ginger root
2 cloves garlic, finely chopped
½ cabbage, finely shredded
2 fresh green chillies, finely chopped
  or blended
1 teaspoon ground turmeric
2 teaspoons cumin seeds
¼ cup lemon juice**

Bring water to the boil. Add onion, ginger
and garlic. Reduce heat, cover and
simmer for 5 minutes. Add cabbage,
chillies and turmeric and mix well. Cover
and simmer for 15–20 minutes. Dry-fry
cumin seeds until they smoke. Sprinkle
over cabbage. Pour over lemon juice and
serve.

Serves 4–6

LASSI

A perfect refreshing drink to serve with
spicy food.

**1 cup low-fat yoghurt
2 cups iced water
2 tablespoons apple juice
  concentrate
few drops rose essence
3–4 ice cubes**

Blend all ingredients and serve.

Serves 4–6

CHILLI CHUTNEY

**2 large very ripe tomatoes
4–6 cloves garlic
3 × 2.5 cm (1 in) pieces fresh ginger
  root
1 fresh red chilli
1 small white onion
freshly ground black pepper
fresh mint, for garnish**

Roughly chop tomatoes, garlic, ginger,
chilli and onion, and blend with pepper in
food processor. Serve garnished with
fresh mint.

Serves 4–6

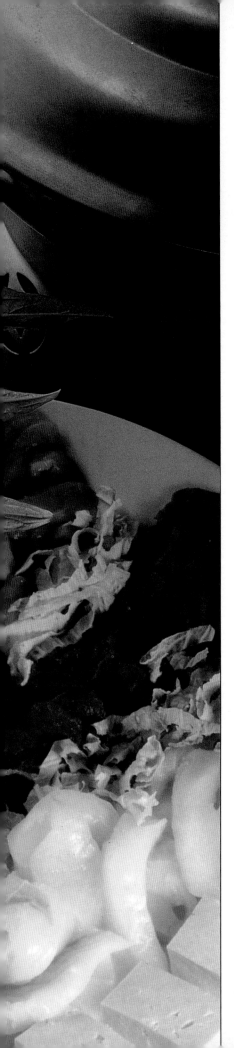

PRITIKIN-STYLE CHINESE CUISINE

Chinese cooking is one of the great cuisines of the world. The Chinese also have a very low incidence of heart disease, attributable to their low-fat diet, so Chinese dishes make a wonderful addition to Pritikin-style cooking.

The main secret is to stir-fry quickly in a non-stick pan or wok, using stock or water, not oil. Pork, often used in traditional dishes, can also be replaced by lean beef, chicken, seafood or vegetables.

Avoid using prepared sauces such as plum, oyster, sweet and sour, lemon, black bean and chilli. You can easily make these sauces at home using fresh, natural ingredients.

Finally, none of my recipes use monosodium glutamate. Many people are allergic to it, and if you are using the freshest produce available, you don't need a 'flavour enhancer'.

BASIC CHINESE CHICKEN STOCK

1 chicken, skinned
2 garlic cloves, chopped
1 tablespoon chopped fresh ginger root
1 medium-sized white onion, roughly chopped
1 carrot, roughly chopped
2 stalks celery, roughly chopped
4 coriander stalks
freshly ground black pepper
6 cups water

Cover all ingredients with the water and bring to the boil. Simmer covered very slowly for 1½ hours to produce a concentrated flavour. Pour soup through a sieve and place liquid in the refrigerator. Later, skim off fatty surface and strain to eliminate all traces of fat.

To make basic Chinese beef, fish or vegetable stock, replace the chicken with 3 cups chopped beef, fish or mixed vegetables. Freeze stock for later use.

Serves 4–6

A selection of fresh vegetables and meats for Mongolian Hot Pot

MONGOLIAN HOT POT

This traditional steamboat recipe is usually cooked at the table in a charcoal-heated firepot. If a firepot is unavailable, a heatproof bowl and gas burner, or electric frypan, can be used. The joy of this dish is that any fresh ingredients can be used. This list of ingredients should serve only as an outline. Vegetarians can use any seasonal vegetables.

100 g (3½ oz) cellophane (bean thread) noodles
2 litres (8 cups) defatted chicken stock (see recipe)
300 g (10 oz) firm fish fillets, cut into bite-sized pieces
300 g (10 oz) beef fillet, thinly sliced
300 g (10 oz) chicken breasts, skinned and thinly sliced
400 g (13 oz) spinach, trimmed and roughly chopped
400 g (13 oz) Chinese cabbage, roughly chopped

Soak cellophane noodles in hot water for 20 minutes. Drain and cut into short lengths. Bring stock to the boil on the stove and transfer 6 cups of it to the firepot. Keep it at boiling point by placing hot coals in the base of the firepot.

Each person cooks his own portion of fish, meat or chicken, using either a wire spoon or chopsticks. Various sauces — soy, chilli, ginger, soy/mustard — should be placed in small containers in front of each person. Dip food into sauces before eating.

When all the meat has been devoured put vegetables, noodles and bean curd into the simmering rich stock. Add remaining stock. Cover and simmer for 10 minutes. Then enjoy the delectable flavours of this amazing soup to round off your Mongolian hot pot/steamboat meal.

Serves 4–6

CHICKEN AND SWEET CORN SOUP

4 cups fresh corn niblets
6 cups basic Chinese chicken stock (see recipe)
300 g (10 oz) skinned shredded chicken
1 medium-sized white onion, chopped
1 clove garlic, finely chopped
1 teaspoon finely chopped fresh ginger root
freshly ground black pepper
3 heaped tablespoons cornflour mixed with 3 tablespoons cold water
3 egg whites
3 diced shallots and salt-reduced soy sauce, for garnish

Shred 2 cups corn niblets in blender. Bring stock to the boil and add all ingredients except egg whites, shallots and cornflour mix. Reduce heat and simmer for 8 minutes. Add cornflour. Simmer and stir for a further 4 minutes. Swirl through egg whites. Garnish with shallots and serve with a small amount of salt-reduced soy sauce.

Serves 4–6

Chicken and Sweet Corn Soup

BEEF IN BLACK BEAN SAUCE

500 g (1 lb) beef fillet, thinly sliced (partially freeze beef for easy slicing)
1 medium-sized white onion, diced
2 cloves garlic, finely chopped
1 teaspoon finely chopped fresh ginger root
1 cup basic Chinese chicken stock (see recipe)
1 tablespoon black beans, soaked in cold water for 15 minutes, drained and mashed
2 tablespoons Chinese wine or dry sherry
2 green capsicums, seeded and cut in strips
1 tablespoon cornflour
1 tablespoon salt-reduced soy sauce

Stir-fry beef, onion, garlic and ginger in ⅓ cup stock over high heat until tender for about 2 minutes. Add black beans and wine to hot wok and stir-fry for 1 minute. Add capsicums to wok and stir-fry for 1 minute. Combine cornflour, soy sauce and remaining chicken stock and add to wok. Simmer about 1 minute until sauce thickens.

Serves 4–6

HOT AND SOUR SOUP

6 dried Chinese mushrooms
1 tablespoon cloud ears (type of mushroom)
5 cups basic Chinese chicken stock (see recipe)
1 fresh red chilli, chopped
200 g (6½ oz) skinned shredded chicken
1 tablespoon finely chopped fresh ginger root
1 cup fresh diced bean curd
1 tablespoon salt-reduced soy sauce
1 tablespoon Chinese wine or dry sherry
2 tablespoons vinegar
1 tablespoon cornflour mixed with 1 tablespoon of cold water
3 egg whites, lightly beaten
freshly ground black pepper
2 shallots, sliced, for garnish

Soak dried Chinese mushrooms in hot water for 30 minutes. Discard stems and slice. Soak cloud ears in hot water for 10 minutes. Discard tough bits.

Bring stock to the boil. Add Chinese mushrooms, chilli, chicken and ginger. Reduce heat, cover and simmer for 5 minutes. Add bean curd, cloud ears, soy sauce, wine and vinegar. Simmer for 2 minutes. Pour cornflour mixture into soup and bring to the boil for 1 minute. Remove from heat and swirl through egg whites. Season with pepper and garnish with shallots.   Serves 4–6

CHICKEN AND MUSHROOM SOUP

5 dried Chinese mushrooms
6 cups basic Chinese chicken stock (see recipe)
300 g (10 oz) skinned shredded chicken breasts
1 tablespoon finely chopped fresh ginger root
2 shallots, sliced
2 egg whites, lightly beaten
2 large lettuce leaves

Soak Chinese mushrooms in hot water for 30 minutes. Discard stems and slice finely. Bring stock to the boil. Add chicken, mushrooms, ginger and shallots. Bring to the boil again, reduce heat and simmer for 5 minutes. Remove from heat and whisk egg whites through soup.

Tear lettuce leaves and place in bottom of individual soup bowls. Ladle hot soup into bowls and serve hot.

Serves 4–6

GINGER TURNIP SOUP

6 cups basic Chinese chicken stock
   (see recipe)
3 cups turnips, peeled and finely
   chopped
2 cloves garlic
1 fresh red or green chilli, finely
   chopped
1 tablespoon finely chopped fresh
   ginger root
3 tablespoons cornflour mixed with 4
   tablespoons cold water
3 egg whites, lightly beaten
freshly ground black pepper
½ cup chopped shallots, for garnish

Bring stock to the boil and add turnips,
garlic, chilli and ginger. Cover and
simmer for 30 minutes. Puree, and return
to saucepan. Add cornflour mixture, egg
whites and pepper. Simmer and stir for a
further 3–4 minutes. Garnish with shallots
and serve.

Serves 4–6

FISH WITH MANGOES

¼ cup basic Chinese chicken or
   vegetable stock (see recipe)
1 teaspoon finely chopped fresh
   ginger root
1 teaspoon garlic, finely chopped
500 g (1 lb) fish fillets, skinned and
   cut into slices
3 fresh ripe mangoes, sliced, for
   garnish

SAUCE
1 tablespoon cornflour
1 cup fresh orange juice
1 tablespoon salt-reduced soy sauce
1 tablespoon Chinese wine or dry
   sherry
freshly ground black pepper

Bring stock to the boil and stir-fry ginger
and garlic for 1 minute. Add fish pieces
and stir-fry for 4 minutes. Remove from
heat.
   To make sauce, combine cornflour
with orange juice. Add remaining sauce
ingredients. Bring to the boil in a small
saucepan. Reduce heat and simmer,
stirring, for 2 minutes until sauce
thickens.
   Return fish to wok or frypan. Heat
through and pour sauce over fish. Top
with sliced mangoes and serve.

Serves 4–6

STEAMED WHOLE SZECHUAN FISH

750 g (12 oz) whole fresh fish
   (whiting, perch or snapper)
3 shallots, chopped
3 dried Chinese mushrooms, soaked
   in hot water for 30 minutes; halve
   caps, discard stems
1 tablespoon finely chopped fresh
   coriander, for garnish

SAUCE
1 tablespoon finely chopped fresh
   ginger root
2 fresh red chillies, sliced
1 tablespoon salt-reduced soy sauce
2 tablespoons vinegar
2 tablespoons Chinese wine or dry
   sherry
freshly ground black pepper

Place fish on heatproof plate and sprinkle
with shallots and mushrooms. Combine
sauce ingredients and pour over fish.
Steam for 10–15 minutes until fish flesh is
white and flakes. Garnish with fresh
coriander.

Serves 4–6

Steamed Whole Szechuan Fish

STEAMED GINGER PRAWNS

300 g (10 oz) fresh uncooked prawns, shelled and deveined
1 tablespoon finely chopped fresh coriander, for garnish

MARINADE
2 tablespoons finely chopped fresh ginger root
2 teaspoons salt-reduced soy sauce
2 tablespoons Chinese wine or dry sherry
2 garlic cloves, chopped
¼ teaspoon Chinese five spice powder

Mix marinade ingredients and marinate prawns for 30 minutes. Place on a heatproof dish. Transfer to a bamboo steamer and steam vigorously for 7–8 minutes. Serve hot or cold garnished with fresh coriander.

Serves 4–6

STIR-FRIED SQUID WITH BROCCOLI

500 g (1 lb) squid, washed and cleaned
¾ cup basic Chinese chicken stock (see recipe)
1 tablespoon finely chopped fresh ginger root
2 cloves garlic, chopped
300 g (10 oz) broccoli, sliced diagonally
2 red capsicums, seeded and cut into thin strips
2 teaspoons cornflour
1 tablespoon salt-reduced soy sauce
2 tablespoons Chinese wine or dry sherry
4 shallots, diced

Slit squid body lengthways and lay out flat. With a sharp knife make shallow cuts on the inside in a crosshatch diamond pattern. Cut the squid into 4 cm (1½ in) squares.

In a wok or frypan, combine 2 tablespoons chicken stock, squid, ginger and garlic and stir-fry over high heat for 2 minutes. Remove squid. Add broccoli, capsicum and another 2 tablespoons stock to the wok and stir-fry over low heat for 3 minutes.

Mix together cornflour, remaining stock, soy sauce and wine. Add to wok, bring to the boil and simmer for 1 minute. Return squid, add shallots and simmer until heated through. Serve hot.

Serves 4–6

STEAMED WHOLE CRAB

2 medium-sized crabs

MARINADE
2 tablespoons Chinese wine or dry sherry
1 tablespoon finely chopped fresh ginger root
3 cloves garlic, finely chopped
2 teaspoons salt-reduced soy sauce
3 shallots, chopped

Remove the hard top shells from crabs and chop each crab into 6 pieces. Remove inedible portions. Chop off claws and crack shell with back of Chinese chopper. Break legs into pieces.

Place crab pieces in a deep heatproof bowl. Combine marinade ingredients, pour over crab pieces and marinate for 30 minutes. Transfer heatproof bowl to bamboo steamer and steam vigorously for 15–20 minutes. Serve immediately.

Serves 4–6

Stir-fried Squid with Broccoli

Spring Rolls with a dipping sauce

SPRING ROLLS

For a vegetarian meal, use mixed sliced vegetables instead of chicken.

10–12 spring roll wrappers (or use filo pastry sheets cut into 20 cm (8 in) squares)

SPRING ROLL FILLING
250 g (8 oz) chicken breasts, skinned and finely sliced
6 shallots, finely diced
200 g (6½ oz) fresh bean sprouts
3 dried Chinese mushrooms, soaked in hot water for 30 minutes; finely slice caps, discard stems

MARINADE
1 tablespoon salt-reduced soy sauce
2 tablespoons Chinese wine or sherry
2 teaspoons finely chopped fresh ginger root
2 garlic cloves, finely chopped
freshly ground black pepper
1 fresh red chilli, chopped

SAUCE
1 tablespoon basic Chinese chicken stock (see recipe)
1 tablespoon Chinese wine or dry sherry
2 teaspoons cornflour mixed with 1 tablespoon cold water

Preheat oven to 200°C (400°F). Combine marinade ingredients and marinate chicken for 15 minutes. Add chicken to preheated wok or frypan and stir-fry for 2–3 minutes. Add shallots, bean sprouts and mushrooms and stir-fry for 2 minutes.

Mix sauce ingredients together. Add to wok and stir until sauce thickens. Allow mixture to cool. Drain off excess liquid.

Divide mixture into 10–12 portions and place one portion in centre of spring roll wrapper. Fold over sides and roll up into parcel. Bake in oven for 30 minutes until golden brown. Serve with a dipping sauce (see recipes).

Serves 4–6

LEMON CHICKEN

500 g (1 lb) chicken breasts, skinned and thinly sliced
fresh lemon slices, for garnish

MARINADE
2 teaspoons salt-reduced soy sauce
3 tablespoons basic Chinese chicken stock (see recipe)
2 tablespoons Chinese wine or dry sherry
freshly ground black pepper

SAUCE
¼ cup fresh lemon juice
¾ cup fresh orange juice
½ teaspoon grated lemon zest
2 teaspoons cornflour mixed with 1 tablespoon cold water

Combine marinade ingredients and marinate chicken for 15 minutes. Combine all sauce ingredients and bring to the boil in a small saucepan. Reduce heat and simmer, stirring, for 2 minutes until sauce thickens. Set aside. Bring marinade juices to the boil in hot wok or frypan. Add chicken and stir-fry for 5 minutes until chicken is cooked. Stir in lemon sauce and simmer for 1 minute. Garnish with lemon slices and serve.

Serves 4–6

LOBSTER WITH BLACK BEAN SAUCE

3 garlic cloves, finely chopped
1 tablespoon black beans, soaked in
   cold water for 15 minutes, drained
   and mashed
2 fresh red chillies, finely chopped
4 tablespoons basic Chinese chicken
   stock (see recipe)
500 g (1 lb) fresh uncooked lobster
   meat, chopped into bite-sized
   pieces
1 tablespoon chopped fresh ginger
   root
4 shallots, finely chopped

SAUCE
2 tablespoons basic Chinese chicken
   stock
2 tablespoons Chinese wine or dry
   sherry
1 teaspoon cornflour
freshly ground Szechuan pepper

In a hot wok or non-stick frypan, stir-fry
garlic, black beans and chillies with 4
tablespoons stock for 1 minute. Add
lobster pieces, ginger and shallots and
stir-fry for a further 3–4 minutes until
lobster is cooked. Combine sauce
ingredients and add to wok. Simmer for
2 minutes until sauce thickens. Serve hot.

Serves 4–6

Villeroy and Boch Black Pearl plate

Lobster with Black Bean Sauce

PINEAPPLE CHICKEN WITH TANGERINE PEEL

This is a fantastic dish to serve for a
dinner party or buffet.

1.5 kg (3 lb) chicken, skinned and
   chopped into 16–20 pieces
2 tablespoons chopped fresh ginger
   root
4 tablespoons dried tangerine peel,
   soaked in hot water for 20 minutes
   and drained
3 tablespoons chopped fresh
   pineapple
2 tablespoons salt-reduced soy sauce
1 cup basic Chinese chicken stock
   (see recipe)
2 tablespoons Chinese wine or dry
   sherry
freshly ground black pepper

Preheat oven to 180°C (350°F). Place all
ingredients in a casserole dish and cover.
Cook for 30 minutes. Remove cover and
cook for a further 10 minutes. Serve hot.

Serves 4–6

RED-COOKED CHICKEN

1.5 kg (3 lb) chicken, skinned
2 tablespoons chopped fresh ginger
   root
1 cup salt-reduced soy sauce
1 cup Chinese wine or dry sherry
2 teaspoons Chinese five spice
   powder
3 cloves garlic, chopped
3 cups water
lemon wedges and parsley, for
   garnish

Truss chicken and place all ingredients in
a large saucepan. Bring to the boil,
reduce heat and simmer for 30 minutes.
Baste chicken during cooking. Turn heat
off and allow chicken to cool in liquid.
   Remove chicken and chop into 16–20
pieces. Arrange pieces attractively on a
platter, garnish with lemon wedges and
parsley, and serve as a cold entree.
Remaining liquid may be used as a base
for soups or sauces.

Serves 4–6

STEAMED CHICKEN AND BROCCOLI

1.4 kg (3 lb) chicken, skinned and
   chopped into 10–12 pieces
2 cups broccoli florets
3 dried Chinese mushrooms soaked
   in hot water for 30 minutes; cut
   caps into quarters, discard stems
4 shallots, chopped, for garnish

MARINADE
1 tablespoon salt-reduced soy sauce
1 tablespoon Chinese wine or dry
   sherry
1 tablespoon basic Chinese chicken
   stock (see recipe)
2 teaspoons finely chopped fresh
   ginger root
2 teaspoons cornflour

Marinate chicken pieces for 15 minutes.
Place marinated chicken in heatproof
dish with marinade, broccoli and
mushrooms on top. Steam vigorously for
35 minutes. Garnish with shallots and
serve.

Serves 4–6

CHICKEN AND SNOW PEAS

400 g (13 oz) shredded chicken breasts
200 g (6½ oz) snow peas, trimmed

MARINADE
1 tablespoon finely chopped fresh ginger root
3 cloves garlic, chopped
1 tablespoon salt-reduced soy sauce
2 tablespoons Chinese wine or dry sherry
1 teaspoon cornflour
freshly ground black pepper
3 tablespoons basic Chinese chicken stock (see recipe)

SAUCE
2 teaspoons cornflour
4 tablespoons basic Chinese chicken stock
1 tablespoon Chinese wine or dry sherry

Combine marinade ingredients and marinate chicken for 15 minutes. Remove stems from snow peas, blanch in boiling water for 1 minute and drain in colander. Place chicken and marinade in heated wok and stir-fry for 3 minutes. Add snow peas and stir for 2 minutes.

To make sauce, mix cornflour with stock and wine. Add to chicken and snow peas. Simmer, stirring continuously, for 2 minutes until sauce thickens. Serve immediately. Serves 4–6

CHINESE CHICKEN WITH PLUM SAUCE

1.4 kg (2¾ lb) chicken, skinned and cut into serving pieces
sliced fresh plums, for garnish

MARINADE
2 cloves garlic, finely chopped
1 teaspoon finely chopped fresh ginger root
¾ cup Chinese wine or dry sherry
1 tablespoon salt-reduced soy sauce
½ cup basic Chinese chicken stock (see recipe)
freshly ground black pepper

PLUM SAUCE
3 teaspoons cornflour
¼ cup fresh orange juice
1½ cups pureed fresh or unsweetened canned plums
2 teaspoons vinegar
1 tablespoon unsweetened apple juice
½ fresh red chilli, finely chopped

Combine marinade ingredients and marinate chicken overnight in refrigerator or for at least 2 hours, before cooking. Place chicken and marinade in casserole, cover and cook at 200°C (400°F) for 30 minutes.

To make sauce, mix cornflour with orange juice. Add to other sauce ingredients and bring to the boil. Reduce heat and simmer for 2 minutes until sauce thickens.

Arrange chicken pieces on serving plate. Sauce can be poured over or used as a dipping sauce. Garnish with plum slices and serve. Serves 4–6

CUCUMBER IN BLACK BEAN SAUCE

3 garlic cloves, finely chopped
1 tablespoon black beans, soaked in cold water for 15 minutes, drained and mashed
1 red chilli, finely chopped
1 shallot, finely chopped
5 tablespoons basic Chinese vegetable stock (see recipe)
2 medium-sized cucumbers, peeled and sliced into discs
2 tablespoons Chinese wine or dry sherry
1 teaspoon cornflour
freshly ground black pepper

Place garlic, black beans, chilli and shallot in non-stick frypan. Stir-fry for 2 minutes with 3 tablespoons of stock. Add cucumbers to frypan and stir-fry for 3 minutes. Combine wine, cornflour and remaining stock. Add to frypan and simmer for 1 minute. Season with pepper and serve.

Serves 4–6

ONION EGG FOO YONG

1 cup basic Chinese chicken stock (see recipe)
6 dried Chinese mushrooms, soaked for 30 minutes in hot water; slice caps, discard stems
6 shallots, finely sliced
1 cup fresh bean sprouts
2 tablespoons salt-reduced soy sauce
7 egg whites, lightly beaten

Bring stock to the boil and add all ingredients except egg whites. Stir-fry for 5 minutes. Swirl through egg whites. Simmer for 2 minutes and serve.

Serves 4–6

BUDDHIST MUSHROOMS

115 g (3¾ oz) dried Chinese mushrooms, soaked in hot water for 30 minutes; cut caps into quarters, discard stems
115 g (3¾ oz) field mushrooms, sliced, discard stems
200 g (6½ oz) straw mushrooms, rinsed and drained
2 teaspoons finely chopped fresh ginger root
3 shallots, finely chopped
3 tablespoons basic Chinese vegetable stock (see recipe)
2 tablespoons Chinese wine or dry sherry
1 tablespoon low-salt soy sauce
2 teaspoons cornflour
1 teaspoon ground pepper

In a non-stick frypan, stir-fry all mushrooms with ginger and shallots in 2 tablespoons stock for 3 minutes. Combine remaining stock, wine and soy sauce with the cornflour. Add to mushrooms, reduce heat and simmer for 2 minutes. Season with pepper and serve.

Serves 4–6

SZECHUAN STEAMED EGGPLANT

1 large eggplant, sliced into discs

SAUCE
4 cloves garlic, finely chopped
3 tablespoons basic Chinese vegetable stock (see recipe)
1 fresh red chilli, finely chopped
1 teaspoon cornflour
2 teaspoons salt-reduced soy sauce
1 tablespoon Chinese wine or dry sherry
freshly ground black pepper

Place eggplant slices on kitchen paper for 20 minutes to absorb bitter juices. Rinse and pat dry. Steam prepared eggplant slices in a heatproof bowl vigorously for 15 minutes. To make sauce, stir-fry garlic in 1 tablespoon stock. Combine remaining sauce ingredients and add to wok or frying pan. Cover and simmer for 2 minutes. Remove eggplant from steamer. Drain, spoon sauce over and serve.

Serves 4–6

CHINESE DIPPING SAUCES

These delicious dipping sauces are ideal accompaniments to spring rolls, Mongolian hot pot meals, vegetable crudites and many more. The fresh ingredients make these sauces especially tasty.

Chinese Vegetable Crudites

SOY/GINGER DIP

4 tablespoons salt-reduced soy sauce
1 tablespoon finely chopped ginger root

Combine and serve.

Makes ½ cup

SOY/MUSTARD DIP

4 tablespoons salt-reduced soy sauce
1 teaspoon Dijon-style mustard

Combine and serve.

Makes ⅓ cup

SOY/CHINESE WINE OR DRY SHERRY DIP

4 tablespoons salt-reduced soy sauce
1 tablespoon Chinese wine or dry sherry

Combine and serve.

Makes ½ cup

SOY/SESAME DIP

4 tablespoons salt-reduced soy sauce
1 teaspoon toasted sesame seeds

Combine and serve.

Makes ⅓ cup

SOY/LEMON DIP

4 tablespoons salt-reduced soy sauce
1 tablespoon fresh lemon juice

Combine and serve.

Makes ½ cup

SOY/PINEAPPLE DIP

4 tablespoons salt-reduced soy sauce
2 tablespoons unsweetened
   pineapple juice

Combine and serve.

Makes ½ cup

SOY/CHILLI DIP

4 tablespoons salt-reduced soy sauce
1 fresh red chilli, finely sliced

Combine and serve.

Makes ⅓ cup

CHINESE VEGETABLE CRUDITES

4 dried Chinese mushrooms
1 cup broccoli florets
1 cup cauliflower florets
2 carrots, peeled and cut into thin
   strips
1 cucumber, sliced
4 shallot curls (see recipe)
6 radish roses (see recipe)
DIPPING SAUCE
2 cloves garlic, chopped
1 tablespoon chopped fresh ginger
   root
¼ cup salt-reduced soy sauce
1 tablespoon toasted sesame seeds
squeeze lemon juice

Presoak Chinese mushrooms in hot water
for 30 minutes. Steam for 10 minutes and
slice in half. Arrange vegetables
decoratively on serving plate. Combine
sauce ingredients and serve with
vegetables.

Serves 4–6

BEIJING FRUIT SALAD

1 cup watermelon balls
1 cup honeydew melon balls
2 cups diced fresh pineapple or
   canned unsweetened pieces
1 cup kiwi fruit circles
1 cup diced apple
2 cups fresh lychees
1 cup sliced fresh mango
2 teaspoons finely chopped fresh
   ginger root
½ clove garlic, crushed (optional)
1 cup fresh orange juice
1 cup unsweetened pineapple juice
fresh rose petals and violets, for
   garnish

Combine all ingredients except garnish.
Chill before serving and garnish with rose
petals and violets.

Note: Fruit salad can be made with any
seasonal fruits.

Serves 4–6

LEMON AND ORANGE TWISTS

Cut a lemon and orange into thin discs.
With a sharp knife cut disc through the
middle up to white pith. Pull both ends of
disc until it twists and place on your
favourite fish, meat, chicken or vegetable
dishes.

SHALLOT CURLS

Remove outer skin of shallot and trim
both ends. Slice the green end into
brush-like strips. Cut down about 2.5 cm
(1 in) into the shallot. Place in iced water
for 10 minutes until the shallot curls.

CARROT CUTOUTS

Peel carrots and cut into thin discs. Use
a special pastry animal cutter to press
into carrot discs, or carve your own
animal shapes with a sharp knife. Flower
petal shapes are also attractive.

RADISH ROSES

Rinse radishes. With a sharp knife, cut
small petal shapes all round each radish,
leaving attached at base. Put in cold
water until flower shape opens.

FRESH FLOWERS

Fresh rose petals, violets and other
flowers can add an artistic touch to
Chinese meals. They look especially
beautiful as a garnish with fresh fruit.

Beijing Fruit Salad

DISTINCTIVE DISHES FROM VIETNAM

Vietnamese food is a particularly good choice if you are following the Pritikin diet, because the emphasis is on very light, low-fat meals. Many dishes are boiled or steamed and always accompanied by side dishes of fresh raw vegetables. Although pork, beef, chicken and duck are served, the portions are very small. Fish is plentiful, and is usually served with rice or noodles, vegetables and fresh fruit.

The main flavouring ingredient in Vietnamese cooking is nuoc mam, a fermented fish sauce. It has a stronger flavour than Chinese soy sauce, enriched by the addition of chillies, garlic, lime juice and vinegar. Use it in minimal quantities, and dilute with water or lemon juice to lessen the saltiness. It is readily available from Asian stores.

PRAWN SOUP WITH RICE VERMICELLI

6 cups fish stock (see recipe)
1 teaspoon grated lemon zest
4 ripe medium-sized tomatoes, roughly chopped
2 cloves garlic, finely chopped
1 tablespoon finely chopped fresh ginger root
2 shallots, chopped diagonally
1 tablespoon Vietnamese fish sauce (nuoc mam)
400 g (13 oz) uncooked prawns, shelled and deveined
100 g rice vermicelli, soaked in hot water for 20 minutes and drained
freshly ground black pepper
1 tablespoon finely chopped fresh coriander, for garnish

Bring fish stock to the boil in a large saucepan. Add lemon zest, tomatoes, garlic, ginger and shallots. Reduce heat and simmer for 5 minutes. Add fish sauce, prawns and rice vermicelli and simmer for a further 5 minutes. Season with pepper and garnish with coriander.

Serves 4–6

BEEF WITH BAMBOO SHOOTS

5 tablespoons defatted chicken or vegetable stock (see recipe)
500 g (1 lb) beef fillet, sliced very thinly (partially freeze beef for easy slicing)
1 cup canned bamboo shoots, rinsed well, drained and sliced
5 shallots, finely sliced
3 cloves garlic, finely chopped
1 tablespoon Vietnamese fish sauce (nuoc mam)
1 tablespoon lightly toasted sesame seeds

Bring three tablespoons stock to the boil, preferably in a wok. Add beef and stir-fry for 1 minute. Remove beef and stock from wok.

Bring remaining 2 tablespoons stock to the boil in the wok. Add bamboo shoots, shallots and garlic and stir-fry for 3 minutes. Return beef and stock to the wok. Add fish sauce and stir-fry for a further 2 minutes. Add sesame seeds to wok and stir until well combined. Serve hot with brown rice.

Serves 4–6

WHITE-COOKED CARROTS WITH SWEET AND SOUR SAUCE

1½ cups basic Chinese vegetable stock (see recipe)
5 carrots, peeled and thinly sliced

SAUCE
¼ cup vegetable stock
2 teaspoons vinegar
4 tablespoons fresh orange juice
2 tablespoons unsweetened tomato juice
2 tablespoons Chinese wine or dry sherry
1 tablespoon cornflour

Bring Chinese stock to the boil. Add carrots, cover and simmer for 10 minutes. Drain and transfer carrots to dish.

Combine sauce ingredients and bring to the boil. Reduce heat and simmer, stirring for 2 minutes until sauce thickens. Spoon sauce over carrots.

Serves 4–6

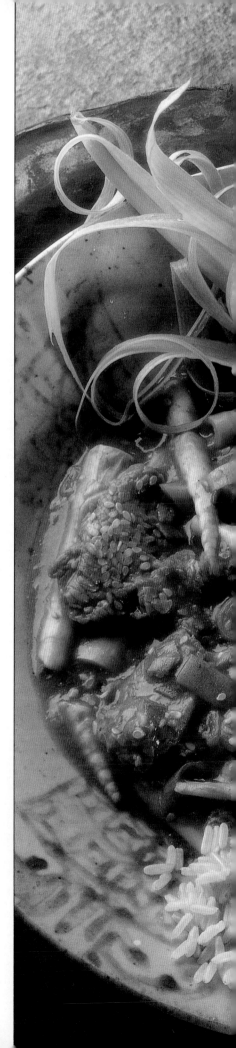

Beef with Bamboo Shoots

STEAMED FISH AND MUSHROOMS

500 g (1 lb) fish fillets, cut into thick slices (choose a firm fish: ling or perch)
8 dried Chinese mushrooms, soaked in hot water for 30 minutes and sliced, discard stems
1 tablespoon chopped fresh ginger root
2 cloves garlic, finely chopped
4 shallots, chopped
1 tablespoon Vietnamese fish sauce (nuoc mam)
100 g rice vermicelli, soaked in hot water for 20 minutes and drained
1 tablespoon chopped fresh coriander

Place fish in a heatproof bowl and cover with the sliced mushrooms. Combine remaining ingredients and pour over the fish and mushrooms. Transfer bowl to a steamer. Cover and steam for 15–20 minutes.

Serves 4–6

CHICKEN AND LEMON GRASS

500 g (1 lb) chicken breasts, sliced thinly
3 cloves garlic, finely chopped
2 fresh red chillies, finely chopped
3 shallots, finely chopped
2 stalks lemon grass, tender part only, finely chopped
freshly ground black pepper
2 tablespoons Vietnamese fish sauce (nuoc mam)
⅔ cup defatted chicken stock (see recipe)
chopped fresh mint and coriander, for garnish

Combine chicken, garlic, chillies, shallots, lemon grass, pepper and fish sauce in a bowl and marinate for 30 minutes.

Add mixture to preheated wok and stir-fry for 5 minutes with 3 tablespoons chicken stock. Reduce heat. Add remaining stock to wok and simmer for a further 15 minutes. Garnish with mint and coriander and serve hot.

Serves 4–6

FAVOURITES FOR ALL OCCASIONS

In this section, you will find easy, healthy recipes to cope with various aspects of modern life: barbecues and outdoor picnics, children's parties, school lunches, Christmas dinners, and entertaining with cakes and desserts. Looking after the family and friends can be fun when you feed them with nutritious, delicious food that you know is good for them.

SENSATIONAL SANDWICHES

Never underestimate a sandwich. It doesn't have to be boring, and you can now buy authentic Pritikin breads, including a spicy fruit loaf and wholemeal rolls.

Avoid using butter or margarine in sandwiches. Herbed low-fat ricotta or cottage cheese spreads, mashed fruit or water-packed salmon or tuna, are delicious alternatives.

Be adventurous! Select from a variety of tasty ethnic cuisines: spicy cold Indian tandoori chicken or prawns, Lebanese hoummos and baba ghanoush, Chinese red-cooked beef or cold herbed Italian pastas.

You can use sandwiches in many ways. Toasted sandwiches, jaffles and grilled Danish open sandwiches are good winter warmers. For dinner parties, attractive pinwheel sandwiches and mini open sandwiches make tempting appetisers.

GOURMET SANDWICH COMBINATIONS

- steamed chicken strips, fresh mango slices, chopped fresh coriander, black pepper
- lean roast beef slices marinated in salt-reduced soy sauce, drained and combined with alfalfa sprouts
- cottage cheese, fresh pineapple slices and chopped chives
- cottage cheese, grated carrot and sultanas
- cottage cheese, blueberries and chopped fresh mint
- mashed banana, seedless grapes and lemon juice
- cooked prawns and paw paw, sprinkled with lime juice
- curried chicken, low-fat yoghurt and chopped fresh coriander
- tomato, onion, mandarin segments and fresh parsley
- chopped dried peaches, cottage cheese and black pepper
- sliced strawberries, ricotta cheese and black pepper
- roast chicken slices, steamed broccoli and dash of salt-reduced soy sauce

PINEAPPLE GINGER SPREAD

2 cups unsweetened crushed pineapple, well drained
1 teaspoon minced fresh ginger root

Combine ingredients and spread on toast or add to seafood sandwich fillings.

Spreads 4 slices bread

SALMON SPREAD

210 g (7 oz) canned water-packed salmon
125 g (4 oz) low-fat cottage cheese
2 shallots, finely chopped
1 tablespoon finely chopped fresh coriander
2 sprigs fresh mint, finely chopped squeeze lemon juice
freshly ground black pepper

Combine all ingredients and mash to a paste. Spread on toast or use as a sandwich filler with cucumber or tomato.

Spreads 4 slices bread

ZESTY CHEESE SPREAD

250 g (8 oz) low-fat cottage or ricotta cheese
1 teaspoon grated Geska cheese
1 tablespoon finely chopped celery
1 tablespoon finely diced radish
¼ cup chopped chives
freshly ground black pepper

Mash all ingredients until well combined and spread onto wholemeal Pritikin bread.

Spreads 4 slices bread

GREAT GRATES

- grated steamed fresh beetroot
- grated raw zucchini
- grated raw pumpkin
- grated oriental daikon radish
- grated raw carrot

Combine with other favourite sandwich fillings.

Gourmet Sandwich Combinations

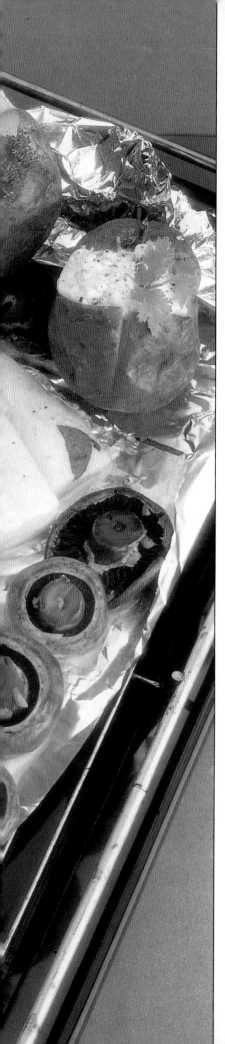

THE GREAT OUTDOORS

Barbecues can be much more than sausages, chops and steaks. Fish, chicken, fruit and vegetables are also great barbecue food and once you have eaten a 'healthy' barbecue, you may have difficulty facing up to a plate of fatty meat and greasy onions.

To extract the best flavours, cook over hot coals not flames, and always preheat the barbecue for an hour before cooking begins.

One-pot cooking is easy: try hearty soups and stews, a precooked vegetable, chicken or beef curry, or pasta. Marinate meat, fish or chicken the day before. Fresh herbs, wine and fruit juice preserve both food and flavour.

HONIARA MARINATED FISH

1 kg firm fish fillets, cut in thick chunks

MARINADE
½ bunch fresh parsley, remove stalks and chop
1 cup dry white wine
2 tablespoons fresh lime juice
1 medium-sized white onion, sliced
1 cup fresh pineapple pieces, pureed
freshly ground black pepper

Marinate fish overnight. Barbecue until fish flakes with a fork. Baste during cooking.

Serves 4–6

DELICIOUS JACKET POTATOES

Prepare 2–3 medium-sized potatoes per person, depending on how much other food is being served.

Sprinkle potatoes with 1 tablespoon of one of the following zesty combinations. Wrap in foil and bake over hot coals for 1-1½ hours. Test with a metal skewer to ensure potatoes are cooked.

TOPPING 1
1 tablespoon finely chopped fresh parsley
1 teaspoon grated Geska cheese
freshly ground black pepper

TOPPING 2
1 fresh red chilli, minced
1 clove garlic, minced
1 teaspoon finely chopped fresh ginger root

TOPPING 3
1 tablespoon finely chopped fresh coriander
1 tablespoon low-fat yoghurt
dash grated lemon zest
freshly ground black pepper

TOPPING 4
1 tablespoon lemon juice
1 tablespoon grated white onion
1 teaspoon finely chopped fresh mint

TOPPING 5
1 tablespoon fresh tomato puree
¼ teaspoon hot paprika
1 teaspoon finely chopped chives

MARINATED MUSHROOMS

500 g button mushrooms, wash and discard stems

MARINADE
2 tablespoons lemon juice
¼ cup fresh orange juice
1 teaspoon red wine vinegar
2 cloves garlic, minced
1 tablespoon finely chopped fresh parsley
freshly ground black pepper

Marinate mushrooms overnight or for at least 2 hours. Barbecue for 5 minutes and serve.

Serves 4

Honiara Marinated Fish, Delicious Jacket Potatoes and Marinated Mushrooms

PEPPERY PUMPKIN SOUP

8 cups defatted chicken or vegetable stock (see recipe)
2 kg (4¼ lb) pumpkin, peeled, seeded and cut into small chunks
2 teaspoons freshly ground black pepper
1 tablespoon finely chopped fresh rosemary or 1 teaspoon dried rosemary
¼ cup low-fat yoghurt

Place stock and pumpkin pieces in a large saucepan. Bring to the boil, cover and simmer for 20 minutes. Stir in pepper and rosemary. Simmer for a further 5 minutes, then mash. Swirl through yoghurt and serve.

Serves 4–6

STEAMED CHICKEN AND TOMATOES

500 g (1 lb) chicken breasts, trimmed of all visible fat and thinly sliced
4 medium-sized tomatoes, chopped
3 shallots, finely sliced
1 tablespoon finely chopped fresh ginger root
2 tablespoons Vietnamese fish sauce (nuoc mam)
freshly ground black pepper
1 tablespoon finely chopped fresh coriander
1 tablespoon finely chopped fresh mint
extra fresh coriander, for garnish

Place all ingredients on a heatproof dish. Transfer dish to a steamer, cover and steam for 25 minutes.
   Garnish with coriander and serve.

Serves 4–6

CHICKEN AND APRICOT STEW

1.5 kg (3 lb) whole chicken
4 cups defatted chicken or vegetable stock (see recipe)
2 medium-sized onions, finely sliced
2 cloves garlic, finely chopped
1 bay leaf
2 stalks celery, chopped
1 tablespoon wholemeal flour mixed with 2 tablespoons of the stock
freshly ground black pepper
1 tablespoon chopped fresh parsley
12 dried apricots

Remove all skin and visible fat from chicken and cut into 6 pieces. Place all ingredients except parsley and apricots in saucepan. Cover and simmer for 45 minutes. Add apricots and parsley and cook for a further 10 minutes. Serve hot with wholemeal bread and salad.

Serves 4

ROSEMARY CHICKEN FILLETS

1 kg (2 lb 2 oz) chicken fillets, trimmed of any visible fat

MARINADE
1 tablespoon finely chopped fresh rosemary or 1 teaspoon dried rosemary
2 garlic cloves, finely chopped
juice 1 orange
1 cup dry white wine
freshly ground black pepper

Combine marinade ingredients and marinate chicken overnight. Barbecue until tender, basting with marinade during cooking. Serve with salad.

Serves 4–6

CHILLI PRAWNS

1 kg (2 lb 2 oz) uncooked (green) prawns

MARINADE
1 fresh green chilli
1 fresh red chilli
1 bunch fresh coriander
½ cup finely chopped fresh mint
6 cloves garlic
juice 4 limes
freshly ground black pepper

Shell and devein prawns, leaving on the tails. Blend marinade ingredients and marinate prawns for at least 2 hours. Barbecue on hot plate or grill for 8–10 minutes.

Serves 4–6

GARLIC ROLLS

6 Pritikin wholemeal rolls
225 g cottage cheese
6 cloves garlic
1 tablespoon chopped fresh parsley
1 tablespoon chopped chives
freshly ground black pepper

Puree all ingredients, except rolls. Cut rolls in half and spread with herb and cheese mixture. Wrap in foil and heat through on barbecue for 15 minutes.

Serves 4–6

WHOLEMEAL CHIVE DAMPER

2 cups wholemeal self-raising flour
¾ cup skim milk
¼ cup chopped chives
freshly ground black pepper

Preheat oven to 200°C (400°F). Sift flour and pour in milk. Combine well. Add chives and sprinkle with pepper. Knead on a lightly floured board for a few minutes and mould into an oval shape.
   Brush top of damper with extra skim milk and bake for 20 minutes until brown.

Serves 4–6

Wholemeal Chive Damper and
Garlic Rolls

THAI CHICKEN FRITTERS

6 chicken breasts, trimmed of all visible fat and pricked with a fork
1 cup wholemeal flour
3 egg whites, lightly beaten

MARINADE
6 shallots
2 fresh red chillies
1 teaspoon chopped fresh ginger root
4 cloves garlic
1 bunch fresh coriander, discard stalks
½ teaspoon grated lemon zest

Blend marinade ingredients, spoon over chicken breasts and marinate for at least 2 hours. Dip chicken into flour, then egg whites and barbecue on hot plate until tender, 10–12 minutes. Serve with brown rice and salad.

Serves 4–6

SIZZLING BEEF WITH BARBECUE SAUCE

1 kg (2 lb 2 oz) beef fillet, trimmed of all visible fat and diced

BARBECUE SAUCE
1 cup red wine
½ cup fresh orange juice
4 cloves garlic, finely chopped
1 teaspoon red wine vinegar
1 tablespoon tomato paste
1 teaspoon paprika
1 teaspoon chopped fresh parsley
freshly ground black pepper

Combine sauce ingredients, place in a pan and bring to the boil. Reduce heat and simmer for 3–4 minutes. Place diced beef on barbecue hot plate. Baste with sauce and sizzle until tender, 10–15 minutes. Pour over any remaining sauce and serve with salad.

Serves 8–10

CRISPY CALAMARI

1 kg (2 lb 2 oz) calamari tubes

MARINADE
1 cup fresh lemon juice
½ cup chopped fresh parsley
1 tablespoon wholemeal flour
6 garlic cloves, minced
¼ cup dry white wine
freshly ground black pepper

Rinse calamari, drain and cut into thin rings. Combine marinade ingredients and marinate calamari overnight or for at least 2 hours. Place on barbecue hotplate or grill and cook for 4–6 minutes until crisp. Serve with salad.

Serves 4–6

CAMPFIRE BEANS

310 g (10½ oz) canned borlotti or cannellini beans
2 cloves garlic, finely chopped
2 medium-sized onions, finely sliced
1 cup defatted vegetable stock (see recipe)
2 very ripe medium-sized tomatoes, roughly chopped
1 tablespoon tomato paste
1 tablespoon fresh sage or 1 teaspoon dried sage
freshly ground black pepper

Rinse beans in colander to remove salt. Place garlic and onions in a large saucepan with stock. Cover and simmer for 5 minutes. Add all other ingredients. Cover and simmer for 15 minutes. Make the night before and reheat in saucepan or frypan over the campfire.

Serves 4–6

BRUSSELS SPROUTS SALAD

1 kg (2 lb 2 oz) small brussels sprouts

DRESSING
2 shallots, finely chopped
½ cup salt-reduced soy sauce
juice 1 lemon
juice 1 orange
2 teaspoons toasted sesame seeds

Steam brussels sprouts until tender. Combine dressing ingredients, pour over sprouts, chill and serve.

Serves 4–6

BEETROOT AND GREEN PEA SALAD

500 g (1 lb) cooked beetroot, peeled and diced
500 g (1 lb) fresh peas, steamed until tender

DRESSING
1 cup fresh orange juice
1 teaspoon red wine vinegar
2 teaspoons finely chopped fresh mint
freshly ground black pepper

Combine beetroot with peas. Pour over combined dressing ingredients, chill and serve.

Serves 4–6

POTATO, CELERY AND RADISH SALAD

½ bunch celery
2 teaspoons black mustard seeds
1 kg (2 lb 2 oz) potatoes, peeled, steamed and diced
8–10 radishes, trimmed and chopped
1 cup low-fat yoghurt
1 tablespoon skim milk

Remove strings from celery and dice. Preheat non-stick frypan. Add mustard seeds and cook until they pop. Off the heat, combine all ingredients, chill and serve.

Serves 4–6

Potato, Celery and Radish Salad

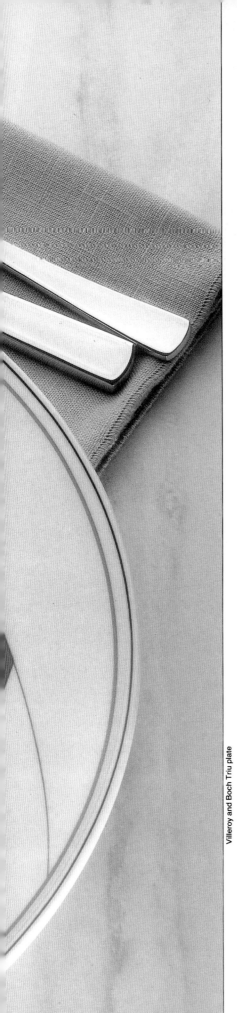

CHRISTMAS CHEER

It is easy to eat a gourmet Christmas dinner without added fat, oil, salt or sugar. The main difference between a rich traditional meal and a low-cholesterol feast is that you won't fall asleep over the plum pudding! Cook and enjoy: turkey with stuffing, roasted vegetables in succulent sauces, Christmas cake and superb steamed pudding.

CHRISTMAS TURKEY

Select a turkey that suits your Christmas lunch or dinner requirements. Remove all skin before cooking.

Choose a tasty stuffing and place inside turkey. Do not pack stuffing tightly because it will expand considerably as the bird cooks.

Wrap turkey in foil. Preheat oven to 200°C (400°F). Place turkey in ovenproof dish and bake for 30 minutes. Reduce oven temperature to 190°C (375°F). Bake for a further 30 minutes. Remove foil and cook for another 30 minutes to brown and crisp the turkey. As a rule, turkeys take 40 minutes per kilogram (15 minutes per lb) to cook.

Allow roasted poultry to stand for at least 15 minutes before carving. Instead of a greasy gravy, serve with a fresh fruit puree or chutney.

SAGE AND RAISIN STUFFING

½ cup cooked brown rice
½ cup homemade Pritikin breadcrumbs
1 tablespoon finely chopped fresh sage or 2 teaspoons dried sage
1 tablespoon raisins, rinsed under cold water and drained
2 tablespoons fresh lemon juice
freshly ground black pepper

Combine all ingredients and stuff into cavity of chicken or turkey. Truss or sew and bake in the oven.

Christmas Turkey served with Herbed Roast Potatoes and Pumpkin, stuffing, peas and cranberry sauce

HERBED ROAST POTATOES AND PUMPKIN

2 tablespoons fresh rosemary or 2 teaspoons dried rosemary
1 tablespoon chopped fresh parsley
6 cloves garlic
freshly ground black pepper
2 kg (4 lb 4 oz) potatoes, peeled and chopped
1 kg (2 lb 2 oz) pumpkin, peeled and chopped into chunks

Preheat oven to 200°C (400°F). Blend rosemary, parsley, garlic and pepper for a few seconds and set aside.

Bake potato chunks in a large ovenproof dish for 40 minutes. Add pumpkin chunks beside potatoes in same dish and bake for a further 20 minutes. Sprinkle over blended herb mixture and bake for a final 10–15 minutes.

Serves 4–6

PRUNE AND ONION STUFFING

1 cup homemade Pritikin breadcrumbs
1 medium-sized white onion, grated
8 pitted prunes, finely chopped
1 tablespoon fresh orange juice
1 tablespoon lightly toasted pine nuts (optional)

Combine all ingredients and stuff into cavity of chicken or turkey. Truss or sew and bake in the oven.

WARM CHRISTMAS RICE

1 cup mixed dried fruit
1 tablespoon fresh lemon juice
¼ cup fresh orange juice
pinch cinnamon
6 cups cooked brown rice, keep warm

Combine fruit, juices and cinnamon in a pan, simmer for 2–3 minutes, stir into rice and serve.

Serves 4–6

BROCCOLI WITH CHEESE SAUCE

1.5 kg (3 lb) broccoli florets, steamed for 5 minutes and set aside
SAUCE
2 cups ricotta or cottage cheese
3 cups skim milk
2 teaspoons grated Geska cheese
1 clove garlic, finely chopped
1 tablespoon chopped fresh parsley
freshly ground black pepper

Blend sauce ingredients for a few seconds and place in saucepan. Heat through, but don't boil. Pour over steamed broccoli and serve.

Serves 4–6

MEXICAN RELISH

This savoury relish is delicious served with roast chicken or turkey, rice, toast, or steamed vegetables.

2.5 kg (5 lb) extremely ripe tomatoes, finely chopped
½ cup white vinegar
¼ cup finely chopped fresh ginger root
12 cloves garlic, finely chopped
1½ cups currants, rinsed under cold water and drained
1 cup grated Granny Smith apple
2 tablespoons tomato paste
½ cup apple juice (not concentrate)
lots of freshly ground black pepper

Combine all ingredients in a large saucepan. Cover and simmer on gentle heat for 45–60 minutes. If there is too much liquid, remove lid for last 15 minutes cooking time to thicken. Pour into jars and seal. Store in the refrigerator.

Makes about 8 cups

BEANS IN SAVOURY SAUCE

1 kg (2 lb 2 oz) French green beans, ends trimmed and cut into short lengths
SAUCE
1 kg (2 lb 2 oz) very ripe tomatoes, chopped
1 tablespoon tomato paste
2 cloves garlic, finely chopped
1 heaped teaspoon mixed herbs
pinch paprika
¼ cup chopped fresh parsley, to garnish

Steam or boil beans until tender. Set aside and keep warm. Combine sauce ingredients, simmer for 15 minutes and pour over beans. Garnish with parsley and serve.

Serves 4–6

STEAMED CHRISTMAS PUDDING

1½ cups pitted prunes
1½ cups homemade Pritikin breadcrumbs
1 cup unsweetened pineapple juice
1 cup raisins
1 cup currants
1 cup mixed dried fruit
½ cup chopped dried apricots
½ cup sultanas
½ cup chopped, well drained unsweetened pineapple pieces
grated zest 1 orange
grated zest 1 lemon
2½ cups wholemeal self-raising flour
1½ teaspoons mixed spice
¼ cup brandy or Grand Marnier liqueur

Cover prunes with water, simmer for 5 minutes, and puree. Combine breadcrumbs and pineapple juice, then add fruit and zest. Stir in flour, spice and brandy. Combine well. Pour into foil-lined 2 litre (3½ pint) pudding basin.

Place pudding basin into large pan. Make sure water is at least half-way up side of pudding basin. Boil vigorously for 4 hours. Be careful not to let pan boil dry; add water progressively.

When cooked, carefully remove from basin and foil lining; wrap well in new foil or baking paper. Store in freezer or refrigerator.

On Christmas Day re-steam for 2 hours. Serve with Ricotta Whip (see recipe) or low-fat yoghurt.

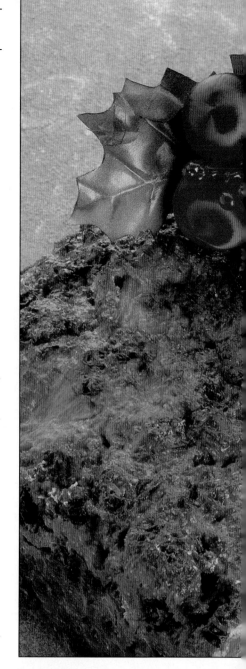

Christmas Cake and Steamed Christmas Pudding

CHRISTMAS CAKE

1 cup sultanas
2 cups raisins
1 cup currants
1 cup mixed dried fruit
½ cup well drained unsweetened
    pineapple pieces
½ cup pitted dates
1½ teaspoons mixed spice
2 teaspoons nutmeg
½ cup brandy
2½ cups fresh orange or
    unsweetened pineapple juice
juice ½ lemon
3 egg whites, stiffly beaten
3½ cups wholemeal self-raising flour

Preheat oven to 190°C (375°F). Place fruit, spices, brandy, orange and lemon juices in saucepan. Slowly bring to the boil. Reduce heat, cover and simmer for 5 minutes. Allow to cool. Fold in egg whites and stir in sifted flour.

Pour mixture into a 22 cm (8½ in) square or round non-stick tin, lined with foil. Cover top of cake with foil and bake for 1 hour. Remove foil and bake for a further 30 minutes. Allow to cool in tin. In warmer weather store in refrigerator.

RICOTTA WHIP

250 g (8 oz) fresh ricotta cheese
¼ cup skim milk
1 teaspoon vanilla essence

Blend all ingredients until smooth. Serve as a topping for desserts. Delete vanilla essence and you have an instant creamy base for pasta sauces.

Serves 4–6

FOOD FOR CHILDREN

Bad eating habits are hard to break, so why not introduce healthy food to your children before they become addicted to fat, sugar and salt? General irritability, fatigue and even tantrums can be induced by a poor diet. You will be surprised how much so-called 'junk food' — potato chips, ice cream, pizza, cakes and biscuits — can be made using healthy ingredients. These recipes are great for parties or after-school munchies and weekend snacks.

FRUIT KEBABS

3 bananas, chopped
250 g punnet strawberries
1 bunch grapes
1 ripe pineapple, thickly diced
6 apricots, halved
3 green apples, chopped
1½ cups fresh orange juice

Thread fruit pieces in an attractive order onto metal or pre-soaked bamboo skewers. Barbecue for a few minutes, basting with orange juice during cooking.

Serves 4–6

SPICY VEGETABLE KEBABS

200 g vegetables per person (zucchini, capsicum, celery, cherry tomatoes, small onions, small chunks of pumpkin, carrot slices)
MARINADE
1 cup low-fat yoghurt
2 garlic cloves, minced
1 teaspoon finely chopped fresh ginger root
1 tablespoon finely chopped fresh coriander
freshly ground black pepper

Combine marinade ingredients and marinate vegetables for at least 1 hour. Thread onto metal or pre-soaked bamboo skewers. Barbecue for 5 minutes and serve with brown rice.

Serves vary

BANANA HOT DOGS

4 fresh Pritikin bread slices
2 tablespoons mashed ricotta cheese
1 teaspoon lightly toasted sesame seeds
4 ripe bananas

Spread bread slices with ricotta cheese. Sprinkle with sesame seeds. Enclose peeled banana, roll up and serve to the nearest child saying: 'I'm hungry!'

Serves 4

CELERY SHARKS

1 bunch celery
2 large carrots, peeled
500 g (1 lb) ricotta or cottage cheese

Remove celery strings and cut stalks into short lengths. Slice carrots into thin discs and cut out orange triangles.
  Stuff cheese into celery lengths. Put carrot triangle (fins) into cheese. Cover serving platter with blue cellophane paper to resemble the ocean. Arrange celery on top and serve.

Serves 4–6

EASY VEGETARIAN PIZZA

1 piece wholemeal pita bread
SAUCE
3 very ripe medium-sized tomatoes
1 small onion, finely diced
1 red or green capsicum, seeded and cut into rings or strips
1 medium-sized zucchini, finely sliced
1 small carrot, peeled and grated
1 cup unsweetened pineapple pieces

Preheat oven to 200°C (400°F). Puree tomatoes and onion and spread mixture over pita bread. Sprinkle with other ingredients. Bake for 15 minutes, slice and serve.

Serves 4

Fruit Kebabs and Spicy Vegetable Kebabs

HEALTHY HAMBURGERS

2 medium-sized zucchini
1 medium-sized carrot, peeled
1 small onion
1 capsicum, seeded
1 very ripe small tomato
500 g (1 lb) lean minced beef or
  cooked mashed potato
freshly ground black pepper
2 egg whites
1 tablespoon chopped fresh parsley
1 cup homemade Pritikin
  breadcrumbs

Chop and blend all vegetables until fine. Add to meat with pepper, egg whites, parsley and breadcrumbs. Form into small patties. Preheat non-stick frypan on high and cook on both sides for 5–6 minutes.

Serve between Pritikin wholemeal rolls with salad of your choice — alfalfa sprouts, tomato slices, shredded lettuce or cabbage — and tomato sauce or chutney.

Serves 4–6

REAL POTATO CHIPS

6 medium-sized potatoes, peeled

Preheat oven to 200°C (425°F). Slice potatoes thinly with a potato peeler. Place in iced water in freezer for 5 minutes, drain and pat dry. Bake in a non-stick oven dish for 15–20 minutes until brown.

Serves 4–6

GREEN RICE SALAD

6 cups cooked brown rice
1 cup lightly steamed broccoli florets
3 shallots, finely chopped
½ cup diced celery
½ cup boiled or steamed fresh peas
1 tablespoon chopped fresh parsley
¼ cup fresh orange juice
freshly ground black pepper

Combine all ingredients and serve.

Serves 4–6

VEGETABLE EGG SCRAMBLE

8 egg whites, lightly beaten
1 teaspoon finely chopped fresh
  parsley
1 tablespoon finely chopped onion
1 tablespoon finely chopped and
  seeded red or green capsicum
¼ cup freshly steamed corn kernels
dash pepper

Combine all ingredients. Preheat non-stick frypan and pour in mixture. Stir around for a few minutes and serve on triangles of toasted Pritikin bread.

Serves 4

SANDWICH MEAT LOAF

2 medium-sized carrots
1 medium-sized zucchini
2 shallots
1 stalk celery
dash tomato paste
1 tablespoon fresh parsley
1 clove garlic
500 g (1 lb) lean minced beef
1 cup grated pumpkin
1 cup homemade Pritikin
  breadcrumbs
2 egg whites

Preheat oven to 190°C (375°F). Chop and blend first seven ingredients. Combine with remaining ingredients and spoon into 28 cm × 10 cm (11 in × 4 in) non-stick loaf tin. Bake for 1 hour. Allow to cool and refrigerate overnight. Slice meat loaf for sandwiches, using Pritikin wholemeal bread.

Serves 4–6

PARADISE DESSERT

3 ripe mangoes; chop off all flesh
pulp from 5 passionfruit
1 tablespoon apple juice concentrate
2 tablespoons low-fat yoghurt
4 peeled oranges, finely sliced

Blend all ingredients except oranges. Pour mixture over oranges, chill and serve.

Serves 4–6

BANANA RAISIN MILKSHAKE

1 ripe banana
1 cup skim milk
1 tablespoon raisins, rinsed under
  cold water and drained
1 tablespoon low-fat yoghurt

Combine all ingredients and blend until frothy.

Serves 1–2

STRAWBERRY MILKSHAKE

1 cup ripe strawberries, hulled
1½ cups skim milk
1 tablespoon low-fat yoghurt
dash cinnamon

Combine all ingredients and blend until frothy.

Serves 2

MUESLI BARS

1½ cups mixed dried fruit
1½ cups raw oats
¼ cup toasted sesame seeds,
  browned in non-stick frypan
½ cup skim milk
1 lightly beaten egg white

Preheat oven to 190°C (375°F). Rinse dried fruit well, drain and pat dry with clean towel. Combine all ingredients and knead mixture together with your hands. Press into flattish square or oblong shape on non-stick baking tray.

Bake for 20 minutes. Cut into bars while still warm. Refrigerate and serve.

Serves 4–6

Healthy Hamburgers and Strawberry Milkshakes

TREATS

My mother was an outstanding cake cook when I was at school. After years of fighting overweight and a high cholesterol level, she adopted the Pritikin eating plan and is now fit, trim and radiantly youthful.

We devised these delicious cakes together. Enjoy them in moderation. Fresh fruit is the ideal sweet snack or dessert. As you look in the mirror or bounce through the day with vigour, you will really feel the rewards of the Pritikin-style of eating.

SPECIAL BANANA CAKE

½ cup cold water
1 cup dates, pitted
25 g (¾ oz) mixed peel, rinsed under cold water to remove excess sugar
150 g (5 oz) cottage cheese
3 very ripe bananas
3 egg whites
1½ cups wholemeal self-raising flour
1 small teaspoon bicarbonate of soda
1 tablespoon skim milk

Preheat oven to 180°C (350°F). Place water, dates and mixed peel in a saucepan. Bring slowly to the boil. Reduce heat and simmer gently for 5 minutes. Allow to cool. Blend mixture with cottage cheese until smooth. Mash bananas and add. Fold in stiffly beaten egg whites and sifted flour. Dissolve soda in milk and slowly fold into the cake mixture.

Pour into non-stick ring or loaf tin and bake for 45 minutes. Allow cake to cool in tin for 5 minutes before turning out onto cake rack. Wrap in foil or baking paper and store in refrigerator.

SPICY OAT LOAF

3 cups raw oats
3 cups mixed dried fruit
1 teaspoon mixed spice
1 tablespoon baking powder
¼ cup low-fat yoghurt
¼ cup apple juice concentrate
1 cup skim milk
1 teaspoon vanilla essence

Preheat oven to 190°C (375°F). Blend oats in food processor until they become fine flour. Rinse dried fruit under cold running water and drain.

Make a well in the centre of the oat flour and pour in all other ingredients. Mix thoroughly and pour into a 28 cm × 10 cm (11 in × 4 in) non-stick loaf tin. Bake for 35–40 minutes. Place on wire rack to cool. Wrap in foil and refrigerate overnight before eating. This cake is best stored in the refrigerator.

APRICOT CAKE

425 g (13½ oz) canned apricots in unsweetened juice
3 cups raw oats
1 tablespoon baking powder
2 egg whites
½ cup skim milk
¼ cup apple juice concentrate
½ teaspoon ground cinnamon

Preheat oven to 190°C (375°F). Drain apricots well and puree. Blend oats in food processor until they become fine flour. Make a well in the centre of the oat flour and pour in all other ingredients. Mix thoroughly and pour into a 28 cm × 10 cm (11 in × 4 in) non-stick loaf tin. Bake for 40 minutes. Place on wire rack to cool.

PINEAPPLE CAKE

500 g (1 lb) mixed dried fruit, rinsed under cold water and patted dry
125 g (4 oz) dried apricots, finely chopped
440 g (14 oz) unsweetened crushed pineapple
¼ cup sweet sherry or fresh orange juice
1 teaspoon mixed spice
1 teaspoon bicarbonate of soda
2 egg whites, stiffly beaten
2 cups wholemeal self-raising flour

Preheat oven to 150°C (300°F). Combine dried fruits, pineapple, sherry and spice in saucepan. Slowly bring to the boil, reduce heat and simmer for 5 minutes. Cool, then add bicarbonate of soda and beaten egg whites. Mix in sifted flour until well combined.

Pour mixture into a lined 20 cm (8 in) cake tin and bake for approximately 1¼ hours. Leave in the tin to cool. This cake is best eaten the following day.

Left to right: Spicy Oat Loaf, Pineapple Cake and Special Banana Cake

FOR YOUR INFORMATION

Glossary of Terms

AUSTRALIA	UK	USA
Equipment and terms		
can	tin	can
crushed	minced	pressed
frying pan	frying pan	skillet
grill	grill	broil
greaseproof paper	greaseproof paper	waxproof paper
paper towel	kitchen paper	white paper towel
patty tin	patty tin	muffin pan
plastic wrap	cling film	plastic wrap
punnet	punnet	basket for 250 g fruit
sandwich tin	sandwich tin	layer cake pan
seeded	stoned	pitted
Ingredients		
bacon rasher	bacon rasher	bacon slice
beetroot	beetroot	beets
bicarbonate of soda	bicarbonate of soda	baking soda
black olive	black olive	ripe olive
calamari	squid	calamari
capsicum	pepper	sweet pepper
caster sugar	caster sugar	granulated table sugar
cornflour	cornflour	cornstarch
cream	single cream	light or coffee cream
crystallised fruit	crystallised fruit	candied fruit
desiccated coconut	desiccated coconut	shredded coconut
eggplant	aubergine	eggplant
essence	essence	extract
five spice	Chinese spice combination of cinnamon, cloves, fennel, star anise and Szechuan pepper	
flour	plain flour	all-purpose flour
glace cherry	glace cherry	candied cherry
green cabbage	white or roundhead cabbage	cabbage
hundreds and thousands	hundreds and thousands	non pareils
icing sugar	icing sugar	confectioners' sugar
pawpaw	pawpaw	papaya or papaw
prawn	prawn or shrimp	shrimp
rock melon	ogen melon	cantaloupe
self-raising flour	self-raising flour	all-purpose flour with baking powder, 1 cup: 2 teaspoons
shallot	spring or salad onion	scallion
snow pea	mangetout, sugar pea	snow pea
sultanas	sultanas	seedless white or golden raisins
tomato puree	tomato puree	tomato paste
tomato sauce	tomato sauce	tomato ketchup
unsalted butter	unsalted butter	sweet butter
wholemeal flour	wholemeal flour	wholewheat flour
yoghurt	natural yoghurt	unflavoured yoghurt
zucchini	courgette	zucchini

If you need to substitute

Fresh fruit: replace with canned or tinned fruit.
Fresh herbs: replace with a quarter of the recommended quantity of dried herbs.
Geska cheese: replace with Sapsago cheese.
Rock melons: replace with honeydew melons.
Snapper: replace with any firm white fish such as haddock, cod or whiting.

Oven Temperatures

	Celsius	Fahrenheit
Very slow	120	250
Slow	140–150	275–300
Moderately slow	160	325
Moderate	180	350
Moderately hot	190	375
Hot	200	400
	220	425
	230	450
Very hot	250–260	475–500

Measurements

Standard Metric Measures

1 cup	=	250 mL
1 tablespoon	=	20 mL
1 teaspoon	=	5 mL

All spoon measurements are level

Cup Measures

1 × 250 mL cup =	Grams	Ounces
breadcrumbs, dry	125	4½
soft	60	2
butter	250	8¾
cheese, grated cheddar	125	4½
coconut, desiccated	95	3¼
flour, cornflour	130	4¾
plain or self-raising	125	4½
wholemeal	135	4¾
fruit, mixed dried	160	5¾
honey	360	12¾
sugar, caster	225	7¾
crystalline	250	8¾
icing	175	6¾
moist brown	170	6
nuts	125	4

PRITIKIN ORGANISATIONS IN AUSTRALIA
Adelaide Dr Malcolm McKay (08) 263 4665   **Albury** Joan Seth (060) 25 1995   **Albert and Logan** Ron Brooks (068) 200 5272
Alice Springs Michael Clancy (089) 52 7595   **Bairnsdale** Bruce Quennell (051) 56 6488   **Ballarat** Alison Sharman
(053) 41 3362   **Bendigo** Lesley Clark (054) 39 5221   **Brisbane** John Gibbs (07) 262 4688   **Bunbury** Brian Kennedy
(097) 21 9018   **Cairns** Megan Hay (070) 51 3125, (070) 55 7472, (070) 55 7480 (A.H.)   **Canberra** Bill Mostyn (062) 65 4126,
(062) 81 4744 (A.H.)   **Colac** Pam Taylor (052) 31 2572   **Echuca** Maureen Skinner (054) 82 3854   **Geelong** Bill Whitehead
(052) 43 2775   **Gold Coast North** Simon Ferrier (075) 35 7450   **Gold Coast South** Geoff Miller (075) 56 0630   **Hobart** Dora
Murray (002) 34 7517   **Lismore** Ken Par (066) 28 2208   **Maryborough** Jim Lyall (075) 46 3580   **Melbourne** Rolet de Castella
(03) 817 4048   **Mornington** Shirley Wallis (059) 89 2643   **Newcastle** Ben Croft (049) 592 2536   **North West Tasmania** Brian
Higgins (004) 31 2320   **Perth** Jonathon Keste (09) 386 5532   **Redcliffe** Claudia Hines (07) 204 5539   **Rockhampton** David
Jenkins (079) 28 7399   **Southern Peninsula** Elida Radig (088) 85 5955   **Sunshine Coast** Eric Barnett (071) 48 5264   **Sydney**
Alex Harris (02) 85 5002, Fred Tross (02) 638 4852   **Toowoomba** Sofie Tod (076) 30 9272   **Townsville** Ann Clemens
(077) 73 3410   **Wagga Wagga** Sally Forsstrom (069) 23 2457   **Warragul/Drouin** Susan Willems (056) 25 1468   **Wollongong**
June Norton (042) 71 2619   **Yarram** Wendy McDonald (051) 85 1357.

Index